ENGLISH
CANALS
EXPLAINED

ENGLISH
CANALS
EXPLAINED

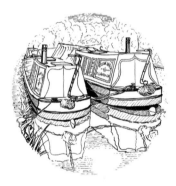

STAN YORKE

COUNTRYSIDE BOOKS
NEWBURY BERKSHIRE

First published 2003
© Stan Yorke 2003
Reprinted 2004, 2006, 2008, 2012

COUNTRYSIDE BOOKS
3 Catherine Road
Newbury, Berkshire

To view our complete range of books,
please visit us at
www.countrysidebooks.co.uk

ISBN 978 1 85306 825 6

Photographs by the author
Line illustrations by Trevor Yorke

Produced through MRM Associates Ltd., Reading
Printed by Cambridge University Press

*All material for the manufacture of this book
was sourced from sustainable forests.*

CONTENTS

Introduction

I f you look at a modern road map, the sort of thing we all carry in our cars, you would be hard pressed to identify many canals. Usually shown as thin blue lines they merge into the general background of rivers and streams. This almost hidden existence is part of the mystery and charm of our canal system. Occasionally glimpsed from a speeding car or a fleeting train, they seem to hide their purpose and extent.

Though obviously affected by years of maintenance work, canals are still basically as they were 250 years ago. The same towpath one walks along today was used by the horses and working boatmen of yesteryear. The locks, bridges and wharfs once alive with working boats are still bustling, albeit now with pleasure boats. This direct link to the past is part of their attraction, a feeling that here is something that has hardly changed since George III was on the throne. The structures themselves blend into the countryside as

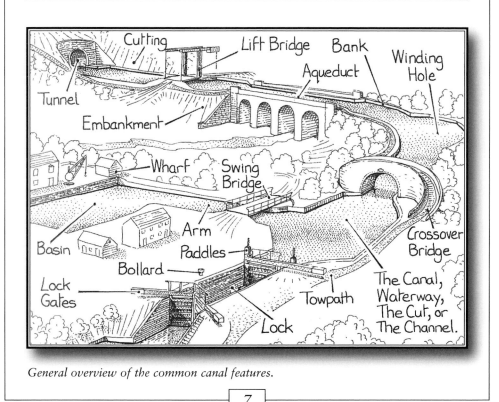

General overview of the common canal features.

Towpath bridge on the Caldon canal at Hazelhurst.

though no more man-made than the trees. All very romantic but we must remember that the canals were born of hard headed commercial needs. That they were built with such grace is simply a reflection of the way in which most utilitarian buildings of their age were constructed.

When boating I often chat to passers by at locks or moorings and the most common question they ask is 'Where can you travel to?'. When I briefly outline the extent of the possible journeys, people are always surprised and intrigued. It was when pondering this casual but genuine interest that the idea of this book came about. Not a technical or historically detailed survey of particular canals, nor just a list of today's facilities – both of which are amply covered already – this is an attempt to link the history and the original workings of the canals to what we can see today. To explain how things work,

Cowroast lock on the Grand Union canal, near Tring, busy with two private narrowboats heading north.

why they are there and how they fitted into the history of our industrial past.

The first section details the history of canals in Britain from the early river navigations of the 17th century through to the renaissance which our waterways are currently enjoying. The second part of the book describes the structures and features you can see while walking or cruising canals today. It is broken down into chapters covering everything from locks, bridges, aqueducts and tunnels down to the very make up of the canal itself. There are numerous photos and easy to understand drawings to help explain how some of these features, like the bewildering lock, actually work. The final section includes suggested sites from around the country which can be visited on foot and, if you are fortunate enough, by boat!

Stan Yorke

Stone ridges on a towpath bridge to aid horses climb and descend. This is at Great Haywood on the Trent & Mersey canal.

SECTION I

A
BRIEF
HISTORY

CHAPTER 1

The Canal Age is Born
1745–1835

FIG 1.1: *An early river bridge, at Great Barford on the Cambridge Ouse. Even today the two navigation arches (just to the left of the lorry) are too dangerous to use when the river is flowing fast.*

History is littered with what can sometimes look like incredible coincidences. Just when the demand for a solution to a problem grew, magically someone came along and invented it; the classic Catch 22 situation where it is not easy to see whether the invention highlighted the problem, or the problem prompted the invention. Certainly the birth of our canal system coincided with some momentous changes in our society but as a brief overview of the times will show it was in fact a slow development of existing transport facilities, though lagging many years behind water transport on the Continent.

If we go back to the 1600s we find a well-established system of roads and navigable rivers, virtually unaltered for hundreds of years. If we look more closely

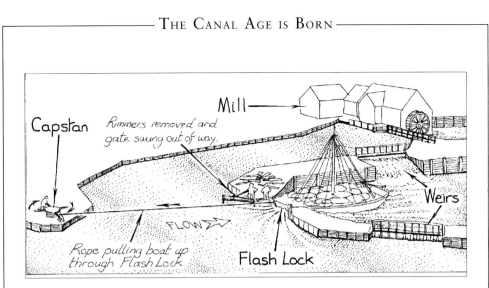

FIG 1.2: *Typical early flash lock. The mill dam would incorporate weirs to allow the passage of the normal river flow as well as feeds to the water wheels. The removable flash lock would be operated only with the mill owner's permission and would be replaced as soon as the boats had passed through.*

at the roads we soon discover that they were only tracks, used by packhorses and horse-drawn carts and coaches. Journeys were slow and could be extremely rough. In winter the roads were either frozen hard or bogged down in mud, and in summer they could be baked rock hard. These difficulties could be tolerated over short distances, for example when produce was conveyed into the local town, but long distance movement of goods was rarely undertaken.

The major rivers like the Thames, Trent and Severn could carry sizeable boats for most of the year and indeed provided the main means of transport for coal, timber and stone. Much of this trade would also use the coast as a way of reaching one river from another. Thus well-established traffic existed between Bristol, Liverpool, South Wales, London and Newcastle. Any heavy products had to be sourced near a good river and were only available to towns on or near a river. Occasionally

heavy loads of timber or stone would be carried beyond these limits by using small flat boats which in the right conditions could be dragged great distances up minor rivers and streams. Normally only undertaken for projects like cathedrals or very large houses this method was slow, labour intensive and relatively expensive. There was also a good import and export trade but, almost by definition, it was always to and from one of the major ports.

There were, however, many problems with moving boats along rivers in addition to the obvious seasonal difficulties. Most had weirs built across them to create mill ponds, which provided a head of water to turn the principal source of machine driving power – the water wheel, used to grind flour and later a part of paper making, fulling cloth and various other processes. On the larger rivers many of these weirs would also have a removable section, often called a flash lock or staunch, which would enable boats to pass

FIG 1.3: *One of only three remaining turf sided locks as used in the earliest river improvements. This one is Walsham flood lock on the river Wey between Pyrford and Ripley, just to the north of Guildford. Today the gate supports are all in concrete but originally would have been timber framing and stone work. The lock chamber would have a stone or wood floor and wood sides for the first 3 or 4 feet. Above this the sides would simply be left as turf covered slopes.*

through. This, however, involved virtually emptying the mill pond to get the water levels similar each side of the weir in order to drag or winch boats through – obviously not popular with the mill owners.

Added to this was the difficulty of passing fords, where local tracks would cross the river, and the early bridges, which were narrow and difficult to negotiate when the river was flowing fast.

Even in London where the Thames was used extensively for passenger transport, the passage under London Bridge was so dangerous in winter that the passengers would disembark, walk around the bridge and reboard the other side, assuming the poor boat crew had survived passing through the bridge arches.

River Improvements

Attempts had been made to improve the passage of boats up and down rivers. A short navigation using three modern 'pound locks' was built in Exeter as early as the 1560s to bypass shallow sections of the Exe. The river Wey, in Surrey, had extensive improvements made in 1651, again involving pound locks which, by using gates at the top and bottom of the chamber, only involved raising or lowering the water the boat sat in, and not a whole length of river.

Other rivers, particularly in Yorkshire, were steadily improved until by the start of the 18th century it had a fairly good waterborne transport system, but only if you were near a river or estuary. You still had to accept that in very wet weather the rivers could be too dangerous and in very dry weather the mill owners would ban the movement of boats in order to preserve their mill ponds.

During this same period there had been a shift in agriculture towards increased production and profit. The enclosure acts created larger fields which enabled the new mechanised sowing and ploughing machines to be better applied, with crop rotation and an appreciation of organic fertilisers all contributing to a better yield. The same period also saw the first embryonic industries being established. In the previous century we had developed steam engines and pumps and everywhere these early machines were making the production of previously hand-made objects easy and cheap. There was one vital ingredient of this change which required transport – coal. Vast quantities were needed and nature had unfortunately put much of it well away from rivers and the sea.

From this particular need was born the canal age. Firstly in Northern Ireland, then to get the St Helens coal to Liverpool and famously in the 1760s to get the coal from the Worsley mines to Manchester.

FIG 1.4: *The two mine entrances at Worsley today. The mine extended for about 40 miles and used the underground waterway to bring out the coal. The mines were worked out by the end of the 19th century but the water channels still provide drainage.*

The Early Canals

This last venture was unique in several ways and has become the school history anchor point for our canal system, though it wasn't actually the first. The Duke of Bridgewater owned mines at Worsley to the north-west of Manchester which supplied coal by conventional methods: drawn up shafts, loaded into carts and taken to the nearest river, in this case the Mersey, and then finally by boat into Manchester along the river Irwell. The greed of the river company in raising charges drove the Duke to seek a more efficient and cheaper method of moving the coal. His agent, John Gilbert, was an experienced mining man who in turn had found an equally experienced millwright – James Brindley.

These three formed a remarkable trio. The Duke had money and knew the right people, Gilbert was ingenious and Brindley understood how to survey water courses and how to keep water where he wanted it. Between them they constructed the Bridgewater canal to take the coal directly from the mine workings into Manchester, where the price of coal subsequently plummeted. Started in 1760, its construction was on a grand scale with two aqueducts and over half a mile of embankments across boggy ground. There was an extension to Runcorn where a large flight of ten locks took boats down to the Mersey and thus to Liverpool.

Partly because of the Duke's standing and partly because of the importance of Manchester and Liverpool, the scheme was closely observed by other industrialists, all very aware of the potential of the new transport system. Thus during the construction of the Bridgewater canal other schemes were proposed and though the movement of coal predominated, many other goods were now involved. Josiah Wedgwood, of Stoke on Trent china fame, wanted to move his products to Liverpool for export and needed better import routes for the china clay which was shipped up from Cornwall. Other entrepreneurs saw the obvious benefits and soon a network of canals was underway. Because Brindley had been involved in the Bridgewater he was seen as the 'must have' man to survey these new canals and so he set out the courses of the narrow canal system that linked the Trent, Mersey, Severn and Thames rivers. At the same time other engineers were building a direct link between the Thames and Severn, plus several other local schemes, all dominated by the movement of coal.

We now see the evolution of two types of canal, loosely referred to as 'narrow' and 'broad'. The narrow canal, that is one to take boats 70 ft long by 7 ft wide, was the creation of James Brindley and great debate has taken place to try and understand why these dimensions were chosen. Brindley was faced with a new problem for his long distance routes – that of obtaining water. When a canal climbs over a hill it has locks on both sides of the summit and, no matter which way the boats are moving, each time a lock is used a lockful of water will descend to a lower level. All this water has to come from the canal summit. Each boat going through a typical Brindley lock uses some 30,000 gallons of water, so to pass up the hill, across the summit and down the other side needs 60,000 gallons per boat! In order to get this water the summit levels need to be able to collect water from streams and reservoirs. The lower down a hill this summit level is, the better the chance of collecting water, and the longer the summit level is, the better it is able to store the water. One way to keep the summits long and low down was to cut tunnels rather than simply climbing to the top and

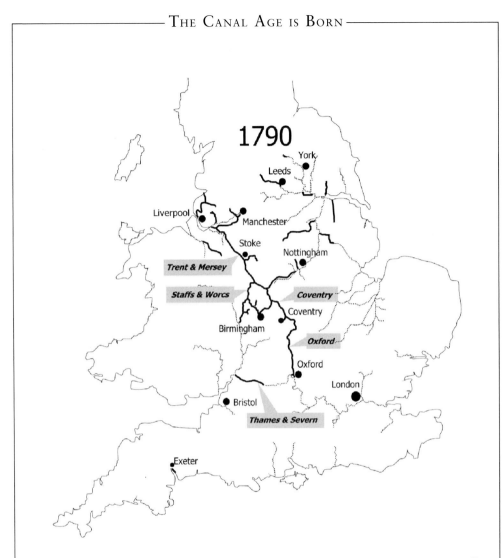

FIG 1.5: *Map of canals as at 1790. Note how the main cities and river estuaries are all now joined and the main coal areas of the Midlands are available.*

down the other side. Tunnel engineering in Britain was still based on mining and a tunnel to pass a boat through was a new challenge; its size, therefore, had to be kept to a minimum. It is probable that the combination of needing to construct tunnels and the obvious water usage in the locks is what influenced Brindley most when setting the boat size, although making the load feasible for pulling by a single horse was also a consideration, as well as the necessity for the boat to negotiate bends (where the canal followed contour lines). We must remember that

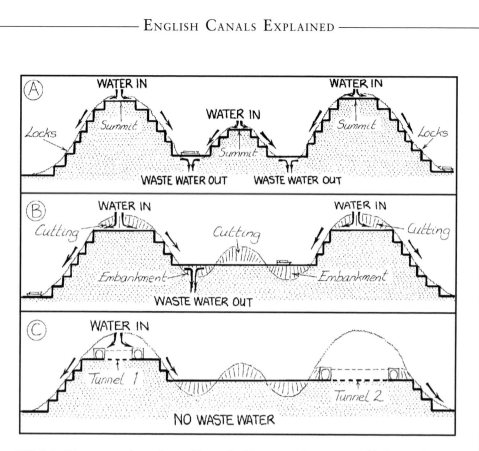

FIG 1.6: *Diagram to show the problem of taking a canal over several hills. 'A' shows the easy and cheap way but where is all that water to come from? 'B' shows the same route but by using cuttings we have reduced the water wastage. 'C' shows the solution that was used in practice. It costs more as it involves cuttings, embankments and tunnels but now there is only one water feed and no wastage.*

the 20 or so tons these boats carried was an immense quantity in an age that had been used to a packhorse carrying, at best, a couple of hundredweight along a rough road.

The broad canals on the other hand were usually built to extend the reach of an existing river navigation further inland. They used the dimensions of the available local river craft to avoid having to exchange goods between boats. Possibly because of the boat building techniques of the day, or possibly because of what could be handled by a small crew, most of these river craft were of similar sizes – something in the 10 to 16 ft wide by 50 to 80 ft long region, which in turn set the sizes for these early broad canals. Long distance links like the Leeds & Liverpool, the Kennet & Avon or the Thames & Severn canals in effect joined river navigations but they produced relatively little through traffic. They had substantial ports at their ends so the import and export trade could reach the coast without using the full length of these cross country routes. They were, however, busy at each end, emphasising the river extension use rather than the long distance canal mode.

The river Severn formed a vital route for materials to and from the Midlands and to serve this two inland ports were built at Stourport and Worcester. These were large areas of safe water where the narrowboats from the Midlands could interchange goods with large river boats which in turn could meet ocean going vessels in Gloucester and Bristol.

Though the broad canals and rivers had barges of variable sizes, the narrow canals had the standard 70 ft by 7 ft boat and these became known simply as narrowboats, though because they are in many ways simply narrow versions of river barges, it is still common to call them barges (however, it must be said that this term is not popular with today's 'narrowboaters' – see chapter 7).

These early canals were all finished by 1790 despite the financial problems caused by the American War of Independence. They were all immediately successful as well, a point not lost on the investors of the day.

FIG 1.7: *Sometimes wealthy landowners would insist on a degree of decoration being used before they would let the canal through their land. This bridge at Cosgrove on the Grand Union is typical of this treatment.*

Later Canals

Proposals for new canals reached a peak in 1793, in which year no less than 24 new schemes were proposed. These later canals had far less luck than the early Brindley canals. Many were backed by people who were looking just for a quick profit, they had no real knowledge of the trade or the likely success of any particular route. All were built during the times of the French Revolution and Napoleonic Wars (1793-1815) which caused widespread lack of money, shortage of men, inflation and a drop in exports. Most canals built in this period suffered all their life from the financial problems of their birth.

The one odd fellow is the canal we know today as the Grand Union, actually an amalgamation of five separate canals. Originally only the Braunston to London section was built to 14 ft wide dimensions, the rest of the route to Birmingham being narrow. It was primarily concerned with getting goods, including coal, into London from the Midlands and not with extending Thames boats inland. It was thus unique in being built to a wide size (14 ft) to enable larger craft to work rather than being built to carry existing river craft. The hope had always been that the narrow northern sections would one day be widened as well, though this had to wait until the 1930s before it was done. The use of 14 ft wide boats was quickly abandoned as there simply wasn't enough room for them to pass each other. The engineers who extended river navigations obviously knew something about the necessary width and depth needed which the Grand Union canal builders didn't! They did, however, allow two narrowboats to share the locks, which helped speed things up.

The sixty years, from 1760 to 1820, that had seen the vast majority of the canal system built also saw the massive movement of people from the countryside to the towns and into the factories. The canals had undoubtedly been a major contributing factor in this growth and, now established, they would continue to serve the needs of industrial Britain.

During the first years of the 18th century tramways had been built, often to bring coal or stone to canal wharfs. The first experiments with a steam engine to haul the trucks had been made and though aware of these tramways, the canal companies did not yet see them as a direct competitor.

By the 1820s, however, the threat of the railways was more apparent and when the immense traffic carried by the canals was taken into account as well, companies sought to make improvements. Two major new routes were built, what we now know as the Shropshire Union main line and the canal. Both were surveyed by Thomas Telford, were built narrow and used the very latest techniques to achieve long direct routes. Locks were grouped together leaving extensive clear stretches in between, all to improve the speed of boat movements. On some other busy sections a second lock was built alongside the original and two major tunnels were duplicated, again to aid traffic flow. At Harecastle on the Trent & Mersey canal, Telford's wider second bore was dug alongside the 1¾ mile long Brindley tunnel. Both were used until early in the 20th century when the older bore became impassable due to mining subsidence. In Birmingham the Netherton tunnel, which had towpaths on both sides and was wide enough for boats to pass with ease, duplicated the older narrow Dudley tunnel. Two new short canals, the Rushall and the Tame Valley, were built to relieve the traffic congestion on the Fazeley canal.

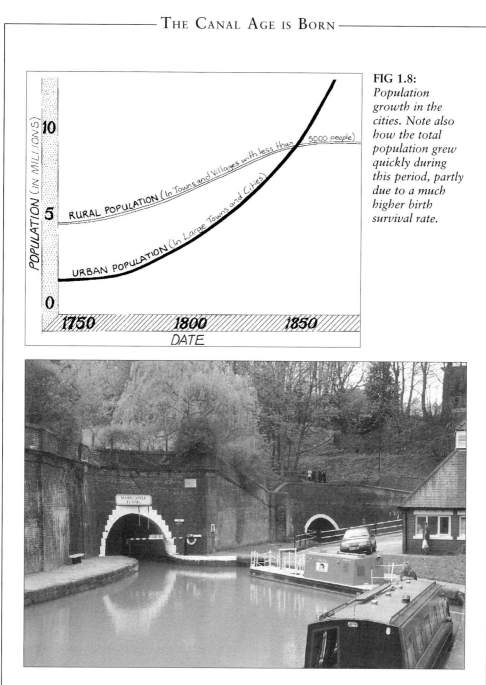

FIG 1.8: *Population growth in the cities. Note also how the total population grew quickly during this period, partly due to a much higher birth survival rate.*

FIG 1.9: *The two Harecastle tunnels. The second Telford bore is on the left, still used today. Brindley's original bore is impassable due to mining subsidence.*

FIG 1.10: *A working boat with early external decoration, based on an engraving by Thomas Shepherd from 1827. Pickford were one of the earliest canal carriers though they gave up canal work in the 1840s.*

By 1835 the canals, which were still seen as the forefront of technology, were thriving. Most were paying dividends, some, particularly the early ones, were paying very handsomely indeed, figures of 25% plus being common. The Loughborough navigation, only 26 miles long, found itself at the centre of a massive coal trade and in 1830 managed a spectacular dividend of 150%. These figures were possible as the canals had little competition. About a fifth of all roads, some 20,000 miles, were now maintained by turnpike trusts, but despite the tolls which were intended to finance improvements, many were still as awful as they had previously been. The rivers had settled down to a steady trade; most were now navigable by good sized craft for the greater part of the year, bridges were wider and weirs were bypassed by modern style locks. The railways were just starting to invade, but their speed and potential wasn't yet evident.

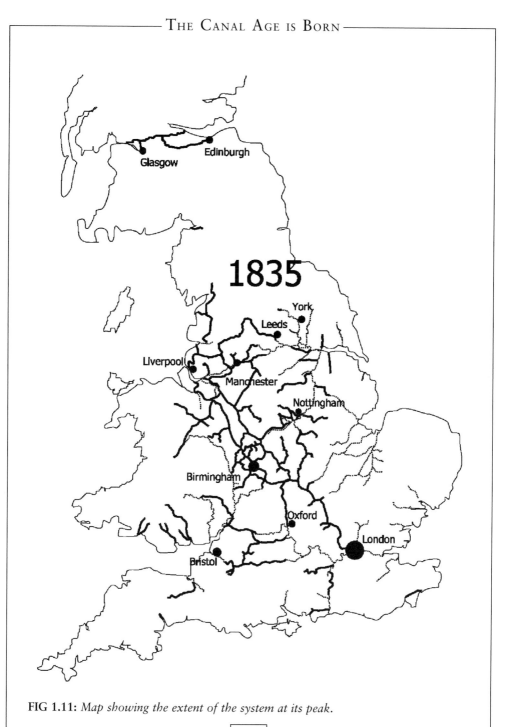

FIG 1.11: *Map showing the extent of the system at its peak.*

Boats in this Period

Under the original Canal Acts, the canal companies were prevented from transporting goods. The Acts also often prohibited towing or delivery services, or the construction of warehousing. The boats were therefore owned and run by separate carriers such as Pickford, who also employed the boatmen. The boats themselves were all wood in construction, as they always had been, and drawn by a horse. The ability of the narrowboats to use both wide and narrow canals made them virtually standard for all long distance work, though some canals like the Leeds & Liverpool had locks too short to take a standard narrowboat. Cabins had been fitted to the boats early on to allow the men to undertake longer journeys which might involve being away from home for several days. These cabins carried the boat's registration number, the name of the owner and the boat's home town, not unlike lorries today.

The boatmen were well paid and were able to maintain a home for their wives and children. By now most villages and towns would have their own wharfs where goods could be loaded and unloaded. These varied from being no more than a level area serving just a small village, to large wharfs with special buildings devoted to particular goods. Life looked very bright indeed for those who worked on the canals!

Summary

The slow and steady growth of technology during the 16th and 17th centuries plus the knowledge gained from early river works had set the scene for the canal age. Prompted by the dramatic effects of agricultural reform and the arrival of steam driven machines, the demand for coal reached a level where something had to change. Despite canal building on the Continent many years earlier, our own efforts started cautiously and not until the Duke of Bridgewater's canal did people realise the potential for the new form of transport. Engineers, like Brindley, Smeaton, Telford and Rennie, had no maps or geological information to help them, no earth moving machines, just their own ingenuity and sweat. In a period of just 30 years they made a massive advance in terms of transport without which the Industrial Revolution would certainly have been hampered. It was now possible to move tons of materials and goods over great distances and to virtually every city in the British Isles. This could be undertaken reliably for almost the whole of the year, and relatively cheaply too. Now the die was cast, the canals worked, they made profits and life on these waterways looked set fair forever. As so often, though, problems were waiting just around the corner.

The cities of Manchester and Liverpool – and greed – again feature in our story. By the 1820s, railways had moved beyond the simple horse drawn tramway affairs which fed minerals to ports or canals for shipment. Viable steam engines had been in production since 1803 and cast iron and then wrought iron rails had improved weight carrying capacity. In 1825 the Stockton and Darlington railway had opened and many hundreds of miles of colliery line were in use. Meanwhile, the Bridgewater canal was now run by a Trust which, along with the River Mersey and Irwell company, had a monopoly on transport between the two cities. In response to the high charges being levied, the tradespeople of Manchester and Liverpool resolved to find an alternative, just as the Duke had done in 1760. They invited the infant railway to provide a new link between them; the rest, as they say, is history.

FIG 1.12: *The statue of James Brindley at Etruria in Stoke on Trent. Note the theodolite emphasising his skills as a surveyor.*

FIG 1.13: *This is the aqueduct over the River Sow, near Milford in Staffordshire, and is typical of the Brindley era. It's so wide that you can't see through the arches. The canal itself, though, is only around 9 ft wide.*

FIG 1.14: *Traces of long abandoned canals can still be found. This section of the Lichfield branch of the Wyrley & Essington canal can still be walked and even the path from the road down to the canal towpath remains.*

FIG 1.15 (top): *This paddle and rimer weir was still in use on the Thames at Abingdon in 1980 but sadly can no longer be seen, having been rebuilt using concrete and hydraulic gears. The flash locks would have been very similar except that the framing and the walkway would have been removable to allow the boats to pass.*
FIG 1.16 (bottom): *The original terminus of the Bridgewater canal at Worsley. The mine entrances are just to the right, past the black and white boarded house. The extension built later towards Leigh and Wigan turns left. Note the 'wide' barges – the Bridgewater was built as a wide canal as it had no tunnels or water supply problems.*

CHAPTER 2

The Long Decline and Renaissance 1835 – 2000

FIG 2.1: *A railway interchange basin. Rail access into industrial areas was limited by the existing structures and factories. These had been purpose built to load to and from canal boats and not trains. Instead the railway companies built interchange basins on the outside of these areas. From here they could transfer goods to and from the canals, which they now owned, and use boats to travel the final few miles to and from the factories.*

The Railway Age

This period of canal history started with great prosperity, the Industrial Revolution was generating enormous quantities of goods, all needing transport. The range of commodities moved by water was vast, though coal still dominated. The railway, however, would not go away. Indeed its growth was faster and more spectacular than that of the canals had been. By 1845 nearly a quarter of the canals had sold out to railway companies. In this one year alone the total mileage of new railways proposed exceeded the total canal mileage! Some companies made good use of their new acquisitions, building interchange basins and exploiting the closely integrated canal system of the large cities. Others simply let their canals die, never to be seen again.

Some canals were used as political pawns. If a rival railway company proposed a line into your territory you could cite your own canals as a reason to keep the newcomer at bay. For example the London North Western railway owned the Shropshire canal network and used it to keep the Great Western Railway almost completely out of Shropshire.

The canals faced this competition in the only way they could, by reducing their rates. This kept the quantity of goods and the number of working boats high but at the expense of profits and dividends. The government tried to help by relieving some of the original trade restrictions that were built into the Canal Acts but not borne by the railways. Thus canal companies could now run their own carrying fleet, deals could be struck with good customers and

FIG 2.2: *Traditional boat decoration. Bold and simple colour schemes were used and, though styles varied, the main components were used throughout the country.*

rate agreements made with the railways. This helped but it didn't stop the overall decline.

Life on the Boats

By the mid 1800s the boatmen faced a simple 'cut costs or no more work' dilemma. They responded by firstly taking on their wives as cheap labour and finally by giving up the land based home and having the whole family on the boat. There were no unions or unemployment money in those days. The carrying companies paid the master of the boat for the mileage travelled and the type of load, from which he had to reimburse his crew and feed the horse. But though the income was now less, the boatman had nobody else to pay, no rent for a family house and just the horse to feed. This was a hard life but it was still relatively well paid and providing work was available these family run boats were very successful. Some boatmen were able to buy their own craft and operate independently; known as Number 1s they were the pride of the canal system. Unfortunately, though, work became harder to get and periods of unpaid waiting became common. These boating families soon took on a life detached from land based people. They worked incredibly long hours in all weathers and raised families in just the cabin of a working boat, that's an area of just 9 ft by 7 ft!

Partly due to the wives' desire to create a real home, the boat decoration now took on a unique art form. Though painted when the boats were in dock for repairs, wonderful decorations incorporating the now familiar roses and castles were the pride and joy of the boatmen. During the 1880s laws were passed to better protect children and as a result a small extra cabin was built at the front of the boats as a second bedroom, often for the children. The only access was a hatch in the roof and these additions were not well liked.

Continued Decline

By reducing maintenance to a minimum and paying lower wages to the boatmen, the canal companies lingered on. In the 1860s steam tugs were introduced and then in the 1870s and 80s steam engined boats appeared which were able to pull a second boat, called the butty, and were thus able to carry greater loads in one journey.

Some idea of the extent of the drop in profits can be seen in the dividends of the Warwick and Birmingham canal company:

FIG 2.3: *Traditional working boat engine controls mounted near the hatch. This craft has a Bolinder engine which used a separate clutch control, a throttle, a forward/ reverse and an oil control valve, making four controls in all!*

1838	15.5%
1843	8%
1845	2%
1851	0.75%
and thereafter	0%

This rate of decline was typical for much of the system though one or two of the older companies, like the Coventry and Oxford canal companies, paid a small dividend right through to nationalisation in 1947.

Despite the gloom there was still some new building. Though not a canal in the 'stroll along the towpath' sense, the Manchester Ship canal was built in the 1880s to allow sea-going ships to reach the centre of Manchester rather than unload in Liverpool – partly to cheapen the costs of moving goods between those same two cities, yet again! This period also saw the construction of the short Slough arm west of London and the New Junction canal bypassing part of the river Don in Yorkshire. There were also improvements made to existing canals to reduce travelling time especially at notorious bottlenecks. Two famous examples, the Anderton lift in Cheshire and the Foxton inclined plane south of Leicester, were both built in this period (see figs 4.27 and 4.28).

The Early 20th Century

The dawn of the 20th century saw the introduction of diesel engines into the boats and by the late 1940s horse towing had virtually vanished. These engines were not, however, the 'turn the key and go' type we associate with modern cars, they were slow running brutes. The first to gain acceptance were the Swedish built Bolinder single cylinder semi diesel engines which needed a blow lamp to start them. These were hand started and which way they chose to turn wasn't too certain either! The speed was regulated by a brass turn wheel and the simple forward, neutral and reverse gearbox was controlled by a lever. Thus the speed and direction of the boat could not be changed quickly and these early diesel powered boats needed considerable skill to manoeuvre.

With the development of the diesel engine came the arrival of the lorry and along with it a vast improvement in the quality of roads. At first lorries were used by both the railway and the canal companies to provide local deliveries and collections. Very soon, though, the road network grew and before long both the railways and the canals faced their final competitor. Partly due to the transport needs of the two world wars and schemes to relieve the high unemployment of the 1930s, the canals managed to hang on. But by the 1950s the end looked in sight. Many canals had been abandoned during the first half of the century and those left were in a pretty poor state.

After the Second World War the mood was one of almost superman style, all concrete, fast roads and tower blocks. It's easy to criticise the dreadful mistakes of the time but we must remember that following the war there was a terrible shortage of housing and possibly a subconscious desire to turn our backs on the recent past. All thoughts of preserving the old were banished. Some might well suggest that the Ministry of Transport was bought out by the road lobby, as the railways also suffered from neglect and lack of investment during this time. Like the railways, the canals had been nationalised and by 1953 were under the control of the British Transport Waterways division of the British Transport Commission. In 1963 the British Waterways Board was created, taking over control of most of our inland system. Known today simply as British Waterways it has gone through many growing pains, being constantly hounded by pressure

FIG 2.4: *These stables at Bunbury on the old Chester canal survived the end of horse towing as they were taken over for use as a boat building shed. Fortunately the outside was left unaltered.*

groups who feel that it is all PR and marketing hype. Nevertheless, today's canal system is in better condition than for many years. The canals have always been a commercial enterprise and have always been changing, adopting the latest ideas to improve profits.

This long period of decline involved many generations of boatmen and their families. No one generation saw the fall from start to finish as has happened more recently in the steel and coal industries. Fortunately for historians, photography started recording the canal scene in the 1870s and with first hand recollections from some of the last working boatmen, our museum industry has been able to reconstruct and display much of this now vanished commercial world.

The Renaissance

Despite the gradual extinction of commercial traffic on canals in the 1950s and 60s there were a few individuals who saw a new role for them. Fighting through weed ridden waterways and negotiating leaky locks, pioneers like Tom Rolt and Robert Aikman were determined not to let the system rot and die. Along with others they had formed the Inland Waterways Association in 1948, which led numerous campaigns to save canals from closure. During the second half of the century growing prosperity meant that more people formed boat clubs, took canal holidays and generally enjoyed mucking about on water.

The result was as close to a near miss as it's possible to have. Canals, lined up to be

FIG 2.5: *A boat club on the southern part of the Grand Union Canal, formed in the 1950s and still thriving today.*

closed and buried, were saved at the last moment thanks to these early pioneers. They had invented the modern pressure group – slowly and steadily they influenced politicians until the concept of canals moved from a place to dump rubbish to a politically desirable leisure location. This movement has not only secured those canals that struggled into the 1950s, but has caused the rebuilding of many closed and lost canals. Some 400 miles and over 500 locks have been restored in the last 30 years, a quite remarkable achievement. The work is still ongoing with several long closed canals due for restoration. There have even been new canals built and a completely new line has been proposed between the Grand Union canal and the river Ouse in Bedford.

The greatest changes have taken place in our cities where water has at last been rediscovered as a virtue. Most well-established cities developed their early industries around the canals which provided for the first large scale movement of materials and goods. These industries were invariably the first to cease work, superseded by imported goods or more modern processes. Their buildings, however, linger on in so many of our towns, run down and none too attractive. These areas make prime sites for civic redevelopment and most, thankfully, have made the canal a feature as well. Walk around the centre of cities like Birmingham, Bristol, Reading, Chester and Sheffield and you can see what can be done when the will is there.

One interesting by-product of restoration work has been the move

FIG 2.6:
Restoration work on the Ashton canal in Manchester in the 1970s. The backbreaking work of clearing these long deserted canals was mainly undertaken by volunteers organised by the Waterways Recovery Group.

FIG 2.7: *Banbury town centre today. In the 1970s this was all fields with just one small boatyard. This yard has been preserved as a museum and workshop in the centre of the redevelopment area just beyond the moored boats.*

towards authenticity. Aided by research carried out in museums, there is now great interest in understanding how things looked, worked and were constructed. British Waterways now tries to use original designs and materials wherever possible and, in parallel with this, a movement has slowly developed in what one might call the artistic side of canals. Authentic boat painting and decoration is being pioneered by people like Tony Lewry and Ron Hough and traditional rope work for fenders and decoration is being produced locally and often on board a boat. Artists like Harley Crossley and Garth Allen have helped to form the Guild of Waterway Artists, which promotes high standards and tries to capture the past of the canal system as accurately as possible.

Summary

The arrival of the railways robbed the canal system of its summer and hastened the winter of its life. At first there was so much traffic that both were kept busy. The railways improved in speed and range at a phenomenal rate and within a couple of generations the canals had entered a twilight existence with the boatmen and their families enduring a hard life that we can barely imagine. Thanks to these hardy workers and the early pioneers of the leisure use of the canals, the canals survived into a more enlightened age. With the aid of modern museums plus the general public access to the network we can now see this history in comfort and admire the ingenuity and beauty of this part of our industrial heritage.

FIG 2.8: *Bulborne works, on the Grand Union, dating from 1848 with a tower added later to hold a water tank. This is one of the three workshops where lock gates are made.*

FIG 2.9: *The Hatton locks just north of Warwick are on part of the Grand Union canal, which was widened in the 1930s. Looking through the typical concrete bridge one can see the new wide lock and, to the right, the old narrow lock now used as an overflow weir.*

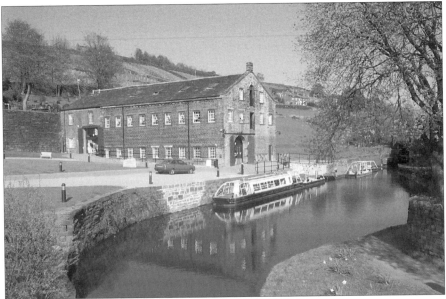

FIG 2.10: *This beautifully restored warehouse on the Huddersfield canal has had a very chequered career. Originally built as a transhipment shed for use during the 16 years that the Standedge tunnel was being built, it then became a railway to canal interchange building but after the 1840s was largely unused. Now back in full use as the Standedge visitor centre near the eastern end of the tunnel (see also fig 5.22).*

FIG 2.11 (above): *The Oxford canal was dramatically improved in the 1830s. This view, at Brownsover, a suburb of Rugby, shows where the old course veered to the right to follow the contours whilst the new route went straight onto a long embankment.*
FIG 2.12 (below): *The National Indoor Arena near Farmers Bridge junction in the centre of Birmingham. This area probably contains more public friendly canalside development than anywhere else in the country.*

The top lock at Hazelhurst on the Caldon canal.

SECTION II

THE
CANAL SYSTEM
TODAY

CHAPTER 3

The Waterway

The canal itself is simply a waterproof ditch, the dimensions of which were influenced by the size of craft that were to use it – not very romantic until you add the water and boats! The trench that was to become the canal was dug, or formed in the case of embankments. It would then be lined with a clay or loam 'puddle' mixture which would make it waterproof. This lining varied across the country dependent on local materials and could be several feet thick if the underlying soil was very porous. There is a lovely story of how Brindley was called to Parliament to

explain just why the water in a canal wouldn't soak away. He took suitable clay and water with him to Westminster and worked the clay to form a bowl into which he duly poured the water. It didn't leak, thus demonstrating to the dubious onlookers that it had become waterproof. These days, apart from where dredging has been done to remove years of silt from the bottom of the channel, you will rarely see anything of this lining. Very occasionally you may notice the top of a modern concrete lining employed to cure a difficult, leaky section such as on the Llangollen or the Kennet & Avon canals.

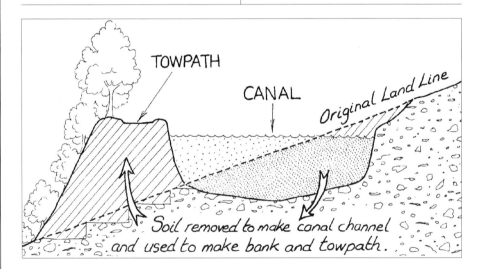

FIG 3.1: *Section through a typical contour canal showing how the ground was used to prevent having to carry soil to or from the site. The canal channel would then be lined with a waterproof layer of puddle.*

FIG 3.2: *Ill-defined but beautiful offside banking typical of many miles of canal where there is no risk of a breach or slippage.*

This modern edging often hides a much more ambitious solution. Sometimes, if fear of slippage is the problem (usually when the canal is on the side of a hill), steel shuttering will have been driven in 15 or 20 ft deep. Where leakage is the problem a butyl liner is placed across the entire canal, rather like a pond at home, then a full concrete lining is poured giving a somewhat unattractive canal but one that doesn't lose water.

Very occasionally the route of a canal was changed, sometimes to replace problem structures, sometimes to accommodate railway or road construction and very rarely to actually shorten the route. Brindley originally built three sets of staircase locks on the Trent & Mersey canal but these soon became a cause of delays and were all rebuilt as conventional individual lock flights. The original routes can still be seen at Meaford locks north of Stone and at the Lawton locks above Kidsgrove. Similarly the remains of the original route of the northern Oxford canal can still be found wandering away from today's long straight sections.

Towpaths

There is one rather obvious feature that makes canals particularly attractive to us today and that is the towing path. Rarely provided on rivers due to land ownership problems, they were fundamental to canals where the movement of boats, up to the late 1800s, was always by means of towing. It's these paths, now extensively

FIG 3.3: *Modern steel piling being driven in along a washed out section of bank. The wooden structure acts as a guide whilst the piles are driven down into the canal bed and then the gap behind is infilled with silt and mud dug up from the canal bed (dredging).*

FIG 3.4: *Modern piling being topped with stonework to give a more attractive finish. The canal here is following a river valley and suffered from slippage. The towpath edge has been strengthened by driving in 15 ft steel piling to prevent further movement.*

FIG 3.5: *Old triangle shaped winding hole and wharf at Brewood, north of Wolverhampton. The wharf is now in use as a hire boat base and boatyard.*

refurbished, that enable us to enjoy and explore the system today, but please remember they are part of the canal and in most cases are technically not public rights of way. The towpaths were normally constructed on the side of the canal where the land was lowest. That side needs a strong bank to prevent slippage and leakage and the towpath bank thus serves two purposes. The canal companies also owned the land on the non towpath side. In order to build the canal they had to purchase a strip of land wide enough for the canal, the towpath and the offside bank. During the decades of neglect the companies failed to mark or maintain these borders. Today we have housing and farmland running down to the water's edge but nevertheless British Waterways own the first metre or so of the land – a source of endless quarrels!

Bank Protection

Wear and tear on the canal sides was anticipated from the start and sometimes a ledge would be deliberately created in which reeds would be planted. This provided a catchment area for soil being washed off the towpath and the plants helped to absorb the impact of the wash from the boats. Many modern boaters complain of these shallow edges, believing them to be due to lack of maintenance, but they have been used from the very beginning.

In the 20th century, due to the greater turbulence of powered craft, the towpath edges have needed reinforcing, firstly with wooden piles, then concrete piles and more recently with galvanised steel. These are tied back to smaller piles driven into the towpath several feet back from the water's edge. Sometimes if the towpath has

FIG 3.6: *This simple overflow weir is unusual as it provides a cobblestone walkway for the horses and a raised path for people, though this pathway was built much later.*

been neglected the top of these tie back piles will show in the middle of the towpath or the tie rods will be exposed.

New piling is usually carried out when the original edging has collapsed and the canal is ill defined. The piles are driven in where the original edge would have been or often slightly further out in order to avoid any stonework still in place below the water line. The resultant area between the new piling and the eroded towpath is then filled with dredgings from the canal, very messy! Later it is seeded and left to dry out. If when walking a towpath you find an unusual amount of bricks and bits of branches in the surface you can be sure that you are walking on dried out dredgings.

The older brick, stone and wooden edging, often well worn, allowed grasses and weeds to grow and hang over into the water, helping the beautiful integrated feel of rural canals. The modern piling is far less helpful to plant life and the galvanised steel piling will probably never be covered over, at least not until it is so rusted that it no longer does its job.

Turning Around

As most working boats were longer than the canal was wide, winding holes, that is a deliberate widening of the canal, were provided for craft to turn around or 'wind' in (this word is usually pronounced with a soft 'i' as in window). They were usually placed near wharfs where boats would load or unload and then need to return in the direction they came from. If you find one today with no commercial

44

FIG 3.7: *This draining sluice has its own railings surrounding the paddle gear standing in the centre with a liftable cover over the water channel and even stop planks to seal off the paddle gear for maintenance.*

buildings nearby it may give a clue to the existence of a long gone wharf. In many places the wharf would be built along one side of a triangular winding hole, thus combining both needs in one place.

Weirs

As much as collecting water for canals was a problem, sudden downpours created an excess that had to be disposed of. Weirs, therefore, have the important function of allowing surplus storm water to run off into local streams. Occasionally you may see a paddle (see fig 3.7), which is usually padlocked, standing on its own beside the waterway. These are part of a sluice which permits the canal to be drained completely into an adjacent stream when there is a need for serious repair work.

Stop Planks

Stop planks and stop gates are used to isolate a section of canal or a lock in order to drain the water out for repair work. A vertical slot is formed at each side of the canal, just outside a lock or at a bridge, into which planks can be lowered until the combined height of the planks is above the water. The lock or canal section can then be drained or pumped out. Storage for the planks themselves varies from untidy heaps or open sheds, to tunnels built into bridges.

Stop planks or gates are also provided at each end of aqueducts or embankments where leakage or a breach would effectively empty miles of canal of water. A modern variation on this is the use of a gate which normally lies flat on the

FIG 3.8: *Cast iron stop plank slot with planks in place. This lock is having new gates fitted and is completely drained. Ashes are normally used plus lumps of turf to achieve a good seal but here expanding foam has been used instead. This shot is on the Macclesfield canal and may well be a trial of this new method of sealing the planks. Note the handles used to lift the planks into position.*

FIG 3.9: *Stop plank 'house' used to store the planks.*

FIG 3.10: *Stop plank 'tunnel' built into a bridge on the Coventry canal.*

FIG 3.11: *Typical flood protection stop gate. This one guards the southern end of the Shelmore embankment on the Shropshire Union canal. It is normally chained open and being on the non towpath side is less of a temptation for younger passers by to fiddle with.*

FIG 3.12: *New piling and the attendant dredging work under way. The dredgings will be smoothed out and seeded to return the towpath to its normal appearance.*

bottom of the canal but can be raised up to provide a seal.

Maintenance

These days most maintenance is undertaken in the winter months to published time schedules. Emergency work is carried out by transporting men and equipment to the site by road. This may seem sad but it enables tools and skills to be brought quickly to a problem and one British Waterways depot can cover many miles of canal. If the problem involves extensive building work then specialist outside contractors are often called in. Apart from emergencies, the regular work involves repairs to bridge and tunnel structures and locks and replacing worn out lock gates.

Among the more common jobs you are likely to see taking place on the canals are dredging and piling the banks. Both activities are carried out throughout the year as other canal craft can usually squeeze past the working boats. In recent years dredging has been neglected due to onerous health and safety requirements covering the disposal of the dredgings. Often these contain minerals from long gone industrial works and BW have to use licensed sites to get rid of the waste. Environmentally desirable as it may be it still adds to the costs and delays the work.

FIG 3.13: *A temporary dam has been constructed to allow the canal to be pumped dry for repairs to the top gate sill and walls on the adjacent lock.*

FIG 3.14: *The same lock site complete with an 'A' frame to lift the gates. The dam is just being built beyond the end of the lock. The new top gate has yet to be put into place and is still waiting for its balance beam to be fitted.*

CHAPTER 4

Going Up, Going Down

FIG 4.1: *General view of a lock showing the main features.*

Locks

The most mechanically interesting feature of our canals is probably the locks. Their job is to raise or lower the course of the canal. Early canals tended to trace the rise or fall of the valley they were following and thus locks occur steadily along the route. Later canal builders tried to keep the locks together in flights, leaving long lock-free stretches in between. Worked

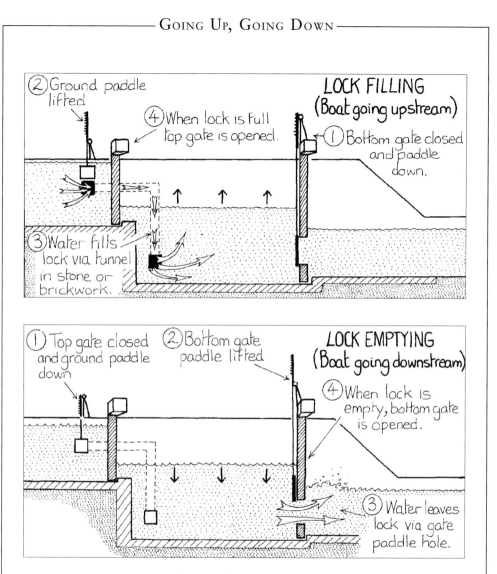

FIG 4.2A AND B: *Diagrams of a lock filling and emptying which will hopefully help explain what goes on! Incidentally, the word 'empty' refers to the lock water being at its lower level and does not literally mean empty.*

with care these flights of locks can move boats along at a surprising speed and provide a place where boaters collect together for a friendly chat.

All locks work in the same way. There are gates at the top and lower end of the lock chamber to hold back the water and then paddles which allow water to be added to the lock to fill it or drained out to empty it. The gates may be single or

FIG 4.3: *This unusual shot of a completely drained canal shows the position where the top ground paddle would normally be and the culvert which the paddle covers over. The culvert comes out lower down and within the lock chamber*

double, sometimes made of steel though wood is the norm. On some rivers the gates take the form of a vertically lifted guillotine. The paddles vary depending on the original designs of the engineer. They are normally operated by a windlass or key, carried by the boater, which enables one to wind up, or down, a toothed rack which in turn lifts or lowers a square paddle below the water line. Sometimes the paddle covers a tunnel, or culvert, which leads between the canal and the lock chamber, sometimes it covers a simple hole in the gate. A ratchet prevents the paddle from dropping down again once you stop winding and these can make a delightful clinking sound as the paddle is raised. Sometimes the paddles and their winding gear are fitted into the top gates, saving the construction of a culvert within the lock walls but giving a dramatic and potentially dangerous water show when opened. Gate paddles are more common on the bottom gates, at the lower end of the lock, where they are usually below the water line. Their use, however, can soon

FIG 4.4A: *The more usual sight, the canal with water in and the ground paddle in place. Not all ground paddle gear is set at an angle like this one on the Oxford canal.*

FIG 4.4B: *Modern paddles, constucted from steel and hard plastics, waiting to be fitted to new gates.*

be seen as the water in the canal immediately below the bottom gates will be turned into a torrent for a few moments when the paddles are raised.

In the 1980s there was concern over the safety of winding gear – the gears are usually open and very basic. This led to the introduction of the unpopular hydraulic paddle gear. They are slow to operate and cannot be quickly closed should a problem arise. Thankfully common sense has prevailed and they are slowly being replaced by traditional designs.

The gates themselves are opened and closed by means of a beam attached to the top of the gate and extending over the adjacent ground. These beams give a good purchase to push or pull the gates and also help balance the weight of the gate itself. Sometimes due to road bridge widening you will find a lock gate beam that has been folded so as to enable the road to come closer to the lock. It is often forgotten just how much water weighs, and trying to open a gate which has not got the water at the same height each side

FIG 4.5: *This lock gear operates a paddle set into the gate and, thankfully, has good reduction gearing to make the job of lifting the paddle easy.*

Stop Lock,
Oxford Canal
by T. Yorke

FIG 4.6: *Some paddle gear is still mounted on a wooden post. Note the pawl (shown raised up) which is dropped onto the winding gear wheel to prevent the rack slipping back down when pressure is taken off the windlass.*

FIG 4.7: *This unusual paddle lifting gear was used on the 1930s widening of the Grand Union canal. It is still mechanical but by using high gearing it enables a very large paddle to be moved, giving faster filling and emptying of the lock. A long rod emerges from the top of the winding gear to indicate if the paddle is shut or open.*

is nearly impossible so patience is needed.

The bottom of the gate post has a round cast metal pin which sits in a socket or pot in the lock sill and provides the turning point for the gate. The top is held back by an iron strap, usually well greased, which holds the top of the gate in place whilst it turns.

When locks are sited close together in a flight, the section of canal between the locks, called a pound, has to hold the water needed to fill the next lock down and to receive the water from the lock above. In small pounds this can result in dramatic changes in level, particularly if someone has operated the locks incorrectly! Failure to realise this can sometimes leave boats stranded on the bottom whilst confused holidaymakers struggle to work out what has gone wrong.

FIG 4.8: *Hydraulic paddle gear fitted to a bottom gate paddle on the Caldon canal. The round drum contains a hydraulic pump which circulates the oil to a ram mounted on the gate which in turn lifts or lowers the paddle.*

FIG 4.9: *Lock beams proudly bearing the name of the canal and the place where they are installed.*

FIG 4.10 (above): *These gate beams have been cranked to allow the road bridge to come nearer the lock for modern road widening.*
FIG 4.11 (below): *The bottom pin (technically called a tan pin) can be seen on the top gate of these old gates waiting to be disposed of after new ones have been installed.*

FIG 4.12: *Steps or stone foot grips are often set into the ground to aid pushing the gates, very useful in wet weather.*

Bypass Weirs

All locks have the facility to pass surplus water down to the next level. This is essential to combat leakage and evaporation. The weirs used to do this vary enormously. Sometimes they are built into the lock itself. Some run water into the lock and only when the lock is full does the surplus water flow over a weir in the lock near the lower gates and down to the pound below. Many lock weirs on the Staffs & Worcs canal are circular and very attractive. This arrangement allows a long weir, the circumference, to be contained in a small area.

Many canals take the water around the locks in open channels, some in mysterious tunnels. Occasionally this ability to pass water down a canal is used to move water continuously, as on the Llangollen canal where water, taken from the river Dee, flows down the canal 24 hours a day and provides water for the North Cheshire Water Board.

Side Ponds

Another feature sometimes seen adjacent to a lock is the side pond. Basically it is just a brick lined pond, originally connected to the lock by a tunnel and controlled by a side paddle. Its purpose was to save water, by passing half of the water from a full lock into the side pond, then closing the side paddle, so that water

FIG 4.13 (above): *Circular bypass weir on the Coventry canal at Atherstone. This shape is common on the Staffs & Worcs canal but, as here, does occasionally turn up in other places.* **FIG 4.14 (below)**: *Side pond still holding water, though no longer used, again at Atherstone.*

FIG 4.15: *The preserved remains of the paddle gear linking duplicated lock chambers at Hillmorton on the Oxford canal.*

could be stored and used later to help fill the empty lock rather than drawing water from the canal above. In practice they were not liked as they slowed the whole process down and today none are in use. Some more complicated versions were used where the side pond was divided into two different levels with two or three separate paddles to play with.

A variation on this was employed where locks were duplicated. Here there would be a tunnel and paddle between the two locks. The idea was that the first half of an emptying lock would flow into the other, empty, lock and provide the first half of a fill. Again they were seen as taking more time and the boatmen did not like using them, despite dreadful

threats from the canal companies if they didn't.

Staircase Locks

One variation on locks as described above is the staircase lock. In these, the bottom gates of one lock are the top gates of the next, in effect two locks squashed together with the pound in between removed. This can sound confusing and indeed their use causes great hilarity to first timers.

They occur in many places, often just two or three locks long, but there are some bigger flights which make interesting viewing. On the Leeds & Liverpool canal, just outside Bingley, there is a flight of five locks. At Foxton there are two flights of five locks though these make clever use of

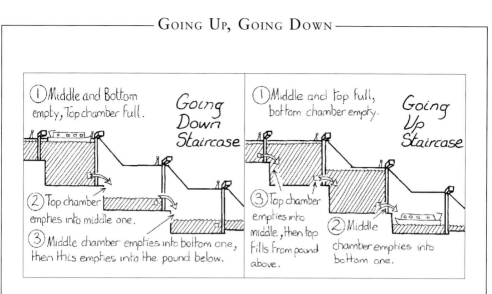

① Middle and Bottom empty, Top chamber full.

Going Down Staircase

② Top chamber empties into middle one.

③ Middle chamber empties into bottom one, then this empties into the pound below.

① Middle and top full, bottom chamber empty.

Going Up Staircase

③ Top chamber empties into middle, then top fills from pound above.

② Middle chamber empties into bottom one.

FIG 4.16 (above): *Diagram of a three lock staircase showing how the flight must be prepared before a boat can set off, up or down the flight.* **FIG 4.17 (below):** *A three lock staircase at Grindley Brook on the Llangollen canal. You can see how the lock we are standing by is separated from the next chamber below by just one set of gates.*

FIG 4.18: *Looking down from the top of the Foxton lock flight near Market Harborough. These were built as two flights of five staircase locks with a small passing pound in the centre. The building on the right is the old boiler house for the inclined plane which now houses a small museum.*

FIG 4.19: *A curiosity can be found on the Staffs and Worcs canal at Bratch where a flight of three locks appears, at first glance, to be a staircase. They are in fact normal locks with the gap between them reduced to just a few feet. The water to and from the lock chambers that would normally be held in these pounds is instead taken via narrow channels to side pounds. The use of side pounds to give greater water storage space between locks in a flight is quite common, though the locks are usually at least 150 ft apart to allow boats to pass each other.*

FIG 4.20: *West of Devizes, the Kennet & Avon canal descends down 29 locks, the central 16 of which form the famous Caen Hill flight. To prevent the water level in the pounds varying too much massive side pounds were provided between each pair of locks.*

side pounds to hold the water. Though only three locks long the staircase flight in Chester is an impressive sight. It was originally five locks long, descending to the river Dee, but this was altered when the arm to Ellesmere Port was built. One of the longest flights in Europe is at Banavie on the Caledonian canal in Scotland where eight locks, known as Neptune's Staircase, rise between Loch Linnhe and Loch Lochy. There is also a five lock flight at Fort Augustus and a further four lock flight at Muirtown near Inverness.

Where only two locks are joined in this way they are strictly speaking called a double lock rather than a staircase but they're just as confusing! Though not at first obvious, a double lock in fact wastes no more water than two separate locks; three or more in a flight, however, do. It's because of the need to prepare the locks when a change of direction occurs. If all the boats were passing in the same direction it wouldn't be a problem but when a staircase flight of three or more locks is prepared for a change of direction, water is wasted. It's this preparation that takes up time as well, making a long staircase a serious bottleneck on busy routes.

Incidentally, when looking at locks today you will often see a ladder set into the side wall. This is a recent feature prompted by health and safety requirements and undreamed of in the old days.

FIG 4.21: *Many locks have name boards as well as number plates.*

Rings, Bollards and Hooks

The other features of locks that can seem strange are the various rings, bollards and hooks that appear littered around them. These were originally involved in controlling the horse drawn working boats. Imagine a loaded working boat approaching a lock – the gates are open and ready but how do you stop the boat crashing into the other end? The horse has ceased pulling long before the craft reaches the lock and will be taking a well earned rest. The answer is in the clever use of ropes, and the rings and bollards strategically placed around the lock. When entering a full lock the back rope was sometimes hooked around a dolly on the end of the top gate. This not only acted

as a brake for the boat but also pulled the top gate closed behind the boat. On locks that didn't have a gate dolly, the front rope would be taken around one of the lockside bollards and used as a brake. When entering an empty lock a crew member would open a top paddle to create a flush of water which stopped the boat's progress and helped slam the bottom gates shut.

Sometimes you will see a small hook set in the stonework beyond the lock gates which was used to help the horse start the boat moving. To give the horse more purchase the towing line ran through a pulley block on the mast. It had a loop at its end which was put over the appropriate ground hook so that the pull from the

FIG 4.22: *Top gate with the round dolly at the end of the lock beam.*

FIG 4.23: *The hook used to help start boats moving, positioned just outside the top gates on the other side from the towpath. As locks get rebuilt these hooks are fast disappearing.*

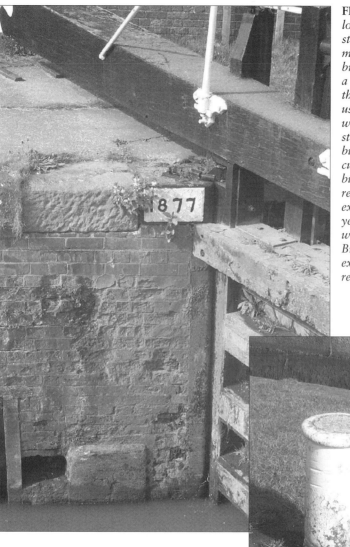

FIG 4.25: *Many locks have a date stone set in the masonry or brickwork next to a gate. These though are not usually the date when the first lock stood on this site but when the current one was built or refurbished. This example shows the year when this wide lock at Braunston was extensively repaired.*

FIG 4.24: *Old cast iron bollard; note the grooves worn by the ropes, particularly near the base. Originally most bollards would have been made of wood.*

FIG 4.26: *Although gates usually have planks and handrails for boaters to walk over them, some had more convenient footbridges added at the lower end of the lock. The boatmen learnt to swing the tow rope under these bridges, catching it as it swung up on the other side.*

horse went via the pulley, giving a two to one advantage and thus helping the horse get started. A toggle in the rope would soon reach the pulley, leaving the horse to take up the full weight of the now moving boat and allowing the rest of the rope to the hook to drop slack. As the boat passed the hook the now slack rope would simply drop off.

Today with most pleasure boats being shorter than the lock chamber there is the danger of the boats being driven to and fro in the lock by the water movement, and so the bollards and rings are used to hold the boats steady by using the ropes.

Despite the remarkably good safety record of locks, those not familiar with

them should exercise caution and in particular keep children from getting too close. An 'empty' lock can easily have a drop of over 10 ft and then another 5 ft of water. If operating a lock then take care with the paddle gear, always make sure the pawl is used and if you lose grip of the windlass, step back and leave it, do not try and stop it!

Lifts and Planes

Locks were not the only solution to getting boats up and down hills. From the earliest days of the 1790s experiments were made with lifts and inclined planes. All the early attempts failed but by the 1830s working lifts were in use in the

FIG 4.27: *The Anderton boat lift in Cheshire following its complete restoration in 2002. Each caisson can carry two narrowboats which including the water weigh in at around 250 tons. The gearing used to lift the caissons when the cable system was used has been left in place on top of the structure.*

West Country on the Grand Western canal, and in Scotland.

Both lifts and planes involved getting the boat into a watertight box or caisson which was then lifted or lowered. This meant making watertight doors which could be opened and closed fairly readily to let the boat in or out but which held the water in place whilst the lift was on the move. Some lifts would carry the boat in an open cradle, thus saving the weight of the water, but this could put unwanted strain on the boat compared to being held in water. Today we are left with only two working lifts, one old and one completely new.

The Anderton lift in Cheshire moved boats between the Trent & Mersey canal and the river Weaver some 50 ft below. There had been interchange here for many years using chutes which enabled salt and other chemicals to be unloaded at the higher level canal and sent straight down into river boats waiting below. The original lift structure, built in 1875, was powered by two hydraulic rams but the high salt content of the river Weaver is thought to have caused corrosion and the rams were replaced by cables and counterbalance weights with electric power to provide the movement. The lift worked until 1983 when the structure was found to be unsafe. Happily it has been completely restored and hydraulic rams once again provide the power. The restoration of the Anderton lift has cost £7 million and trip boats and a visitor centre all add to the site's interest and help pay for the restoration.

The new lift is in Scotland near Falkirk, part of a massive restoration project to bring the Forth & Clyde and Edinburgh & Glasgow Union canals back to life. This lift and three new locks replace a derelict eleven lock flight. Again two caissons are used but they are held between giant curved arms which revolve like a Ferris wheel. This beautiful structure lifts boats almost 100 ft in just 15 minutes! As with the Anderton lift, trip boats and a visitor centre make this a tourist attraction as well as a boating facility. Both these lifts were financed, like most of the major canal restoration works, by a combination of funding including European Union grants. They are expected to create jobs and inject money into the local economies, rather than simply repay their costs.

Traces of some of the other lifts and planes still exist. The biggest inclined plane was at Hobbacott Down on the Bude canal in Cornwall. It had a vertical lift of 225 ft and used tracks like a railway with the weight of the descending boat pulling up the ascending one. These were not full sized boats but tub boats fitted with wheels to suit the inclined planes. This avoided having to make a watertight box or caisson to hold the boat. The power was provided by allowing a tank filled with water to descend down an adjacent well shaft. On reaching the bottom, its job done, a valve would open, emptying out the water ready for the other tank to be filled and descend. Many inclined planes used a water wheel to provide the power, others a steam engine.

One inclined plane, whose remains can still be seen and indeed may one day be restored, was built at Foxton, near Market Harborough, on the Leicester arm of the Grand Union where the ten narrow staircase locks (see fig 4.18) often delayed traffic. The lift was built to take 14 ft wide craft, or a pair of narrowboats, as there had been hopes of widening this route, but that never happened. Again two caissons were used, carried on wheels which ran on sets of rails. Cables connected the two caissons so that the one coming down pulled the other one up. The difference in energy needed was provided by a steam

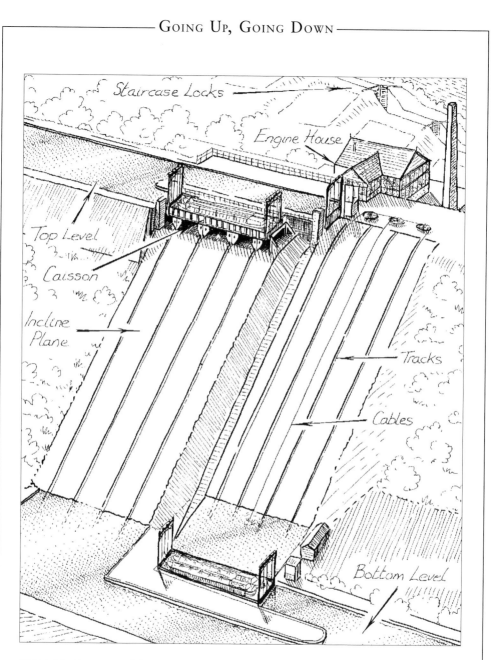

Staircase Locks

Engine House

Top Level

Caisson

Incline Plane

Tracks

Cables

Bottom Level

FIG 4.28: *Drawing of the Foxton incline near Market Harborough. Note the lifting gates at each end of the caissons to enable the water to be retained for the journey. On reaching the top or bottom these gates could be lifted to allow the boats to leave. Similar gates protected the end of the canal at the top end.*

FIG 4.29: *Looking down the Marple flight of locks on the Peak Forest canal. The side arm not only stored water but originally served lime kilns.*

winding engine. The rails, however, were not up to the task and having to keep the steam engine ready 24 hours a day led to its demise. Opened in 1900, it closed in 1910 with the adjacent locks returning to use. There is a small museum on the site with working models showing the entire lift system in its former glory.

Going Over and Under

FIG 5.1: *An original Brindley bridge on the Trent & Mersey canal which apart from minor repairs is believed to be virtually as built.*

Bridges

Probably the most common structure, apart from the canal itself, is the bridge. The style of the older bridges often reflects the original design of the canal, though almost no truly unaltered original bridges exist today. Bridges were provided to allow tracks and, later, roads to cross over the canal. They were usually built with gentle curves which helped to strengthen the bridge but also added beauty.

The traditional brick or stone road

FIG 5.2: *This graceful cast iron towpath bridge was built across the original route of the Oxford canal as part of the 1835 improvements. It now guards the entrance to a marina complex.*

bridges were built long before metalled roads and heavy lorries. As in much of the building work on the canals, local brick would be used or, if available, local stone. Many bridges were originally built to reconnect farmland dissected by the canal. Those which today seem to go nowhere often carried tracks between villages which in turn have vanished. Nearly all such bridges crossed both the canal channel and the towpath to enable the towing horse to continue through the bridge uninterrupted.

Where the towpath had to cross over another canal, for instance at a branch or junction, a simple brick or stone bridge would be used. Wide enough for the horses and not too steep, the pathway would be cobbled and provided with ridges to give the horse grip. After 1810 these towpath bridges were sometimes made from cast iron. Several of these graceful iron bridges can be seen on the northern Oxford canal and in Birmingham.

FIG 5.3: *Classic example of a bridge which has been widened. In this case the 'new' section is wider than the original.*

When the old road tracks grew in size and capacity the bridges became inadequate; they were often widened, sometimes more than once, with the original part ending up just carrying the footpath. Look at the brickwork as you pass under a bridge and you may be able to see the original width and the extension. Eventually a complete rebuild would be needed to cope with the heavier loads and the familiar modern bridge with vertical side walls carrying pre-stressed beams appeared.

Another form of bridge was used when the towpath changed sides. This changeover was sometimes due to geographical reasons, the towpath usually being on the side of the canal with the lowest land. In other cases landowners had decreed that the towpath should not directly connect to their property or grounds. The challenge for the canal bridge designers was to get the towing horse across without interrupting the

FIG 5.4: *This turnover bridge is at Marple, on the Macclesfield canal. We are standing on the towpath which crosses over at this point. The horse walks over the bridge, keeps turning to the right and passes under the bridge. The manoeuvre has not involved taking the towing rope from either the horse or the boat.*

towing process. The solution was the turnover bridge – this almost defies simple description but is obvious once seen.

A similar problem exists at locks where there is often a footbridge across the bottom of the lock. Here a slot would be made across the bridge, allowing the towing rope to pass through. Sometimes the slot would be at one edge of the bridge which was cantilevered over the canal.

Lift Bridges

The simplest and, more importantly, the cheapest over-canal structures are the lift bridges. Many of these are still in use today and though obviously fairly modern versions, they follow the original patterns. Some simply pivot (see fig 5.6) but most have a flat bridge crossing the waterway with a pair of beams above and chains or rods connecting them. When the extended ends of the beams which balance the structure are pulled the bridge lifts. Mostly used on rural canals like the Llangollen, southern Oxford, Stratford upon Avon and Caldon canals, they require the boater to stop and lift them and having passed through to lower them

FIG 5.5: *A centre gap bridge at Lapworth on the Stratford upon Avon canal. These slots haven't been used in earnest for decades and many of them are now too narrow to let a towing rope through.*

FIG 5.6A: *The most basic type of lift bridge, now rare, north of Oxford, which doesn't look as if a boat can pass under – but they do!*

FIG 5.6B: *Conventional lift bridge at Wrenbury on the Llangollen canal. The weight of the bridge is balanced by the weight box at the far end of the overhead beams. The arrangement allows the bridge to be raised to a very high angle, giving a good clearance for the boats.*

again. Ironically these same canals now carry some of the heaviest leisure traffic due to their very pretty rural character. Some lift bridges have been rebuilt to cope with modern traffic and are thus much too heavy for hand operation. These are now operated by hydraulic rams controlled from an adjacent console.

Swing Bridges

A variation on the lift bridge is the swing bridge – these are flat structures which pivot on one side of the canal. Again the same need to open and shut the bridge applies, which made them unpopular with the working boatmen. Sometimes these

structures have become redundant and are left in the open position. Occasionally you will find just the basic stonework remaining where a lift or swing bridge once stood. These bridges were always built on the non towpath side in order to allow a clear passage for the towing rope, a fact that today makes their use awkward as it leaves a crew member stranded on the opposite bank – and makes single-handed boating very difficult too.

Protection Devices

One interesting feature that can still be seen is the protective guards fitted to the corners of bridges to prevent the towing

FIG 5.7 (above): *Modern hydraulic operated lift bridge near Shirley on the Stratford upon Avon canal. This carries a busy roadway and is much too heavy for hand lifting. The controls are housed in a console opened by a special key carried by boaters.*
FIG 5.8 (below): *A hand operated swing bridge being closed after a boat has passed through. This is on the Market Harborough branch of the Grand Union in Leicestershire and represents the largest type of bridge still worked by hand.*

FIG 5.9: *Most bridges, of all types, carry a number plate for identification. Some have their name displayed as well.*

FIG 5.10: *Cast iron bridge brickwork guards used to protect the brickwork from the towing ropes.*

FIG 5.11: *Remains of old roller protectors on the Trent & Mersey in Stone.*

FIG 5.12: *Roller rope guards on the top of a road bridge wall approaching the entrance to a lock. Note the ironwork which guides the rope onto the roller.*

ropes from damaging the brickwork. Usually cast iron they would soon have grooves worn in them by the wet and dust filled ropes. Beware though, towing heavy loads decreased dramatically in the early 1900s and virtually ended by 1940 so any genuine ironwork should be at least 60 years old. You will, however, come across beautiful smooth castings complete with lots of deep grooves, which are modern replicas!

An alternative type of protection consisted of a vertical roller held between two iron brackets bolted to the corners of the bridge. These would have provided a much easier passage for the rope though no doubt the wooden rollers often needed replacing. These were also used at tight corners or junctions to guide the towing ropes.

Iron protection bars and rollers are also often found across the top of bridges by locks where the towing rope would ride up and over the bridge stonework as the boats moved into or out of the lock.

Aqueducts

Aqueducts, where the canal goes over a stream, river or road, are among the most spectacular structures on the waterways yet their impressive scale may not be visually obvious when strolling along a towpath on top. Early aqueducts tend to be squat and lack grace due to the need to carry the canal channel which can require a stonework depth of 7 ft or more plus great width to achieve enough sideways strength. These can be some 30 ft wide, relying on the brute force strength and weight of the structure to hold the canal channel in place. Later aqueducts used iron tie bars to hold the two outer walls together, allowing the structure

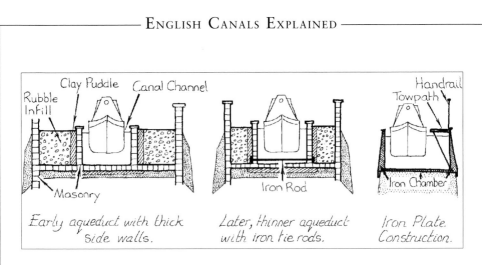

FIG 5.13: *Drawing of cross sections of developing aqueducts. The reduction in width meant less weight which in turn meant greater heights were possible.*

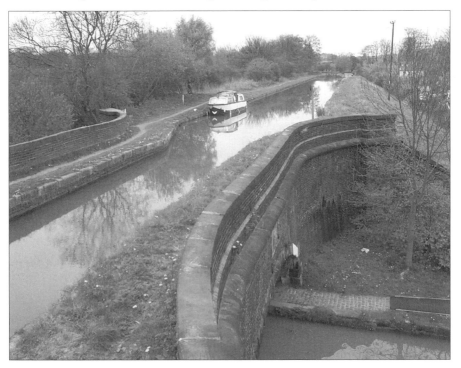

FIG 5.14: *This second generation aqueduct, at the southern end of the Macclesfield canal, is much narrower than the early ones, due to using iron tie rods across the base of the canal to give greater side to side strength.*

FIG 5.15: *This cast iron trough takes the Engine Arm branch over Telford's 'new' main line in Birmingham. In this case the towpath has its own decorative ironwork support, though often the towpath was built over the water channel itself.*

FIG 5.16 (above): *The Dundas aqueduct on the Kennet & Avon canal south-east of Bath – a beautiful example of heavy stone construction. Both the Dundas and Avoncliff aqueducts have recently been repaired to ensure their continued safety.*
FIG 5.17 (opposite): *The Marple aqueduct over the Goyt valley is difficult to show in its full glory but some idea of its impressive size can be gained from this view. Nearly 100 ft high it used iron tie rods to achieve sideways strength without becoming too wide and heavy.*

to be less wide and thus less heavy. This in turn allowed the structure to be made higher as the supporting pillars were holding less weight.

The least heavy solution was a cast iron trough used to hold the canal. Needing no clay puddle or infill, the weight was kept to a minimum and these structures could be supported at heights of over 100 feet.

Occasionally it was desirable, usually in order to preserve a single summit level, to cross a valley not just a few feet above the river but tens of feet, or even a hundred feet. Several superb aqueducts were built using conventional methods. These had to be fairly massive to have sufficient strength; two beautiful examples can be found on the Kennet & Avon canal south-east of Bath. Possibly the best conventional aqueduct carries the Peak Forest canal nearly 100 ft above the Goyt valley near Marple, though due to the

FIG 5.18: *The Pontcysyllte aqueduct. This employs a cast iron trough to carry the waterway over the river Dee. It was designed by Thomas Telford, with advice from William Jessop, and opened in 1805.*

steepness of the valley and tree growth it's not easy to see the full structure. The pillars are pierced by 12 ft diameter circular holes to reduce the weight and strengthen the structure, a technique often used today.

On the Llangollen canal a different approach was used. Of the two aqueducts, the one at Chirk is 70 ft high and used cast iron plates for the canal base. This tied the two masonry sides together and enabled a lighter, narrower structure to be used. At some time in its life this aqueduct seems to have been fitted with a full cast iron trough, that is iron sides as well as the bottom, though it still retains its masonry walls.

Just around the corner, at 127 ft above the Dee valley and over 1,000 ft long, the aqueduct at Pontcysyllte is an awesome site. Even the approach embankment is massive, reaching over 90 ft high before the cast iron trough of the aqueduct leaps across the valley. Here a whole trough was constructed of cast iron plates supported on beautiful slim masonry columns. So superb was the cast iron work and the

FIG 5.19: *This view of the towpath on the Pontcysyllte aqueduct emphasises the reduction in width achieved by using cast iron. The towpath is held on brackets over the water; this allows some room for the water to pass around a boat, which otherwise would not be able to move.*

masonry of the piers that it remains in use today nearly 200 years later, having needed no major repair work at all. The towpath is in excellent order at this end of the Llangollen canal and a walk here includes both aqueducts, although the less brave may want to keep a firm grip on the handrail.

Tunnels

The most difficult structures to build on a canal and ones which claimed the lives of numerous navvies were tunnels. They tend to be either fairly short, simply taking the canal under a local hill, or very long to help achieve a long summit level. The short variety often have towpaths through

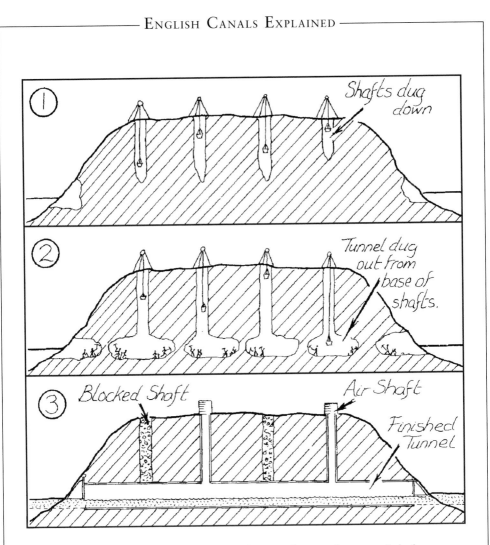

FIG 5.20: *Diagram of tunnel construction showing the way that several shafts were used to provide more tunnelling faces.*

them which can be walked, but beware puddles and water dripping from the roof! The long ones rarely have towpath access, the Netherton in Birmingham being the exception.

Tunnels were constructed by marking out their route, normally a straight line, across the hills. Shafts, approximately every 150 to 200 yards, were then dug down to the anticipated point where the canal tunnel would be. Digging then started out in both directions from the bottom of these shafts as well as from each side of the hill. The accuracy with which these shafts were measured and the correctness of the direction in which the

FIG 5.21: *A rather dramatic piece of maintenance was carried out on the Blisworth tunnel, south of Northampton, in the 1980s where long sections of the original lining were in a poor condition. A modern laser-guided boring machine was assembled inside the tunnel which cut out the old brick lining and replaced it with concrete segments. Nearly a third of the entire tunnel was rebuilt. When finished the tunnelling machine was disassembled inside the tunnel and removed bit by bit. After the work was completed a spare tunnel lining segment was laid outside the southern end of the tunnel for all to see.*

digging went were paramount to achieving a straight and true tunnel, and the kinks in many today show that some were more successful than others!

As you can imagine you couldn't just dig away, the hole you made had to be supported and a brick lining was constructed around the tunnel literally foot by foot as the digging proceeded. Difficult rock would sometimes be encountered which needed blasting to remove, and these sections would be left unlined if the rock was hard and stable. More often though, water and saturated sand would be encountered, giving the tunnellers great problems. Frequently a second smaller

FIG 5.22: *Standedge tunnel on the Huddersfield canal at 5,698 yds long is the longest ever built in Britain. Taking 16 years to construct it has recently been reopened for the passage of boats as part of the restoration of the Huddersfield Narrow canal.*

FIG 5.23: *The eastern portal of the Sapperton tunnel showing the classical style of decoration used. When built in 1789, it was the longest tunnel in the world and hopefully will one day be reopened as part of the Thames & Severn canal restoration.*

FIG 5.24: *One of three steam driven tugs used on the tunnels at the northern end of the Trent & Mersey canal. Note the wheels on the sides to prevent the tug from damaging the tunnel walls – these tunnels have many alarming kinks in them!*

tunnel was cut, either under or to the side of the main one, to take water away. Water pressure building up behind the tunnel walls can still cause problems to this day.

When completed some of the vertical construction shafts would be left open to act as ventilation shafts, the others being capped and filled in. These shafts, with their attendant heaps of soil, can still be spotted over most long canal tunnels.

Working the Boats Through Tunnels

Before the steam tugs, boats had to be legged or poled through tunnels. A few of the later tunnels had towpaths which enabled the horse to carry on towing, once it had been trained to accept the darkness.

Legging involved lying on one's back on a board placed across the boat. The leggers, usually one each side, then 'walked' along the side of the tunnel wall, drawing the boat along. In wide tunnels, such as Braunston and Blisworth, this meant hanging out over the water in order to reach the walls. Often at these wide tunnels there would be full time leggers who just worked boats through that one tunnel, leaving the boat to await a return working at the far end.

Later on, tugs would take trains of boats through. Some tugs had engines with propellers, but most used a winding device to pull themselves along using a chain or cable which lay on the tunnel floor. Later still, electric tugs appeared which picked up their power from a trolley wire set in the roof of the tunnel or used batteries, but they still used a chain or cable laid in the tunnel to pull themselves along.

CHAPTER 6

Canalside Buildings and Structures

FIG 6.1: *The delightful wharf building at the end of the Welford arm of the Leicester section of the Grand Union Canal, built to serve the village and now used by British Waterways. These days the arm provides popular visitor moorings and a marina complex.*

Wharfs

The most common canalside structure is the wharf, or rather was the wharf, since so many have long disappeared. Once a canal was completed and trading, every village or town along its route would build a wharf either next to an existing roadway, or on a newly built track leading just to the wharf. The wharf itself may have been no more than a stone or brick wall at

FIG 6.2: *Typical blocked up arch that once led to a short arm and factory loading areas. The nearer arch is bricked up just the other side of the towpath. These are just two of the dozens of such arms that existed in Birmingham.*

which boats could come in and a fairly clear area where goods could be loaded and unloaded. These wharfs were paid for and serviced by the villagers themselves, though road stone was often carried free of charge by many canal companies to help maintain the tracks. It is the very simplicity of these country wharfs that has enabled them to disappear back into nature so completely once they were no longer needed.

In towns the wharfs would include covered storage areas and more extensive moorings for the boats, often in a widened stretch or even down a separate canal arm. The wharfs would be mainly provided by the town and its traders though both the canal company itself and the major carrying companies would provide wharfage in the larger cities.

A natural extension of the wharf was the private arm which would serve just one or two factories or mines. These were extensive in the big manufacturing cities

FIG 6.3: *The old wharf at Copredy on the Oxford canal. The buildings are still used for a canoeing club and the open area thankfully has not been developed.*

like Birmingham and even today some still exist even if sad and unused. Many of these arms have been filled in and the entrance is only obvious because the towpath bridge is still there, rising and descending for no apparent reason. One or two still remain in use as boatyards or boat moorings. The vast network of meandering branches and arms in Birmingham gave rise to a total mileage that exceeded Venice, though possibly not in quite such romantic surroundings.

Often all that remains of a wharf will be a canalside wall, usually on the non towpath side and about 2 to 3 ft high above the water. The adjacent surface will often still be flat even though possibly completely overgrown. Some wharfs have been built on and only the straightness of the edges gives any clue.

Workshops

All the canal companies built workshops where maintenance and repair work could

FIG 6.4: *The yard at Fradley, on the Trent & Mersey canal, still in use today. The crane came from a basin in Burton upon Trent and was restored by the Tent & Mersey Canal Society. The base for the original crane here can still be seen, just behind the restored one.*

FIG 6.5: *Linesman's hut and store near the top of the Napton lock flight on the Oxford canal.*

FIG 6.6: *Three beautifully restored dry docks at Stone. This site has been used for canal repairs since the very beginning of the Trent & Mersey canal in the 1770s. In the same family hands for over 50 years it is now a popular hire base and boatyard.*

be carried out. Some just served the local area, some undertook lock gate building as well as normal wear and tear repairs. Three such larger depots are still active today, at Bulborne on the Grand Union (see fig 2.8), at Bradley in Birmingham and at Northwich on the river Weaver.

Workshops would have cranes and trolleys to handle and load heavy materials. There would be carpenters' shops, blacksmiths and general storage areas.

Most lock flights have small buildings used to hold materials for maintenance and to give protection from the weather to the canal staff. Many of the longer flights would have a lock keeper's cottage, usually at the top, most of which are still in use today, though now as private houses.

Dry Docks

These were docks, usually covered, where boats and their hulls could be repaired or painted. They consisted of a chamber similar to a lock from which the water could be drained out. This was provided with stout wood beams on the floor, onto which the boat would settle as the water lowered. Such docks were often built at the side of lock flights where the water could be easily emptied to the next pound down the flight.

Signs

Most canals were marked out with mileposts, purportedly to aid the calculation of tolls. Frankly as most traffic moved between physically fixed wharfs or

FIG 6.7: *Mileposts are a common feature with each canal company having their own style. Many are new replicas often provided by the local canal society.*

The National Trust proclaiming the river Wey navigations, which it owns.

FIG 6.9 (above): *Delightful information signs recently provided along the Trent & Mersey canal near Stoke on Trent.*

FIG 6.8 (left): *Modern British Waterways 'post' sign. These are the most common signposts and will be found throughout the canal system.*

FIG 6.10: *Though now rarely seen by the canals, many of the old company signs are preserved in the museums. This one is at Ellesmere Port.*

factories, I'm not convinced of the connection between mileposts and tolls. The boatmen usually knew their routes well and didn't need mileages. Possibly a more likely reason is that they were there so that locations for breakdowns or maintenance could be identified. As many mileposts didn't appear until 40 or 50 years after the canal opened this second reason seems more likely.

Pump Houses

Despite reservoirs, extra water was always needed at the canal summits and back pumping was used from the beginning, usually using steam driven pumps. This involved pumping water from below a lock back up to the pound above the lock. Sometimes it would be pumped around

several locks if they were close together. In addition sometimes traffic would start and end on a canal without crossing the summit at all. The Coventry generated much more local traffic than the Oxford for instance. This meant that there was a need to add extra water along the route of the canal near Coventry as well as at the summit on the Oxford canal.

The problem of summit level water supplies was only really beaten by British Waterways in the 1990s by extensive use of back pumping of water from lower levels to the summits, using modern electric pumps – a situation the early canal companies would have died for!

There are four old pumps that have been restored to working order, three steam driven and one, at Claverton on the

FIG 6.11: *Typical 'local' pump house at Hawkesbury junction outside Coventry. This one was used to raise water from a well shaft and is fast disappearing into modern housing.*

FIG 6.12: *The old pump building at the bottom of the Braunston flight of lock – not the original building but a Victorian rebuild. The adjacent marina uses the reservoirs that were built to provide the pump with water in the dry months.*

FIG 6.13: *A more modern pump house built in the 1940s to pump water up the Grand Union locks heading away from London and towards the summit at Tring.*

Kennet & Avon canal, driven by a water wheel. They are operated on special open days if you want to see them working, but do confirm dates first.

The Claverton pump is driven by two large undershot water wheels (the wheel is turned by water flowing under it rather than from on top) fed by a leet from the river Avon that once fed a grist mill. This water wheel then drives pumps which lift 100,000 gallons of water an hour from the river to the canal 47 ft above. The whole site and the pumps have been restored by the Kennet & Avon Society with help from Bath University. An electric pump now performs the routine pumping but on special weekends the water driven pump is run.

At Crofton, again on the Kennet & Avon, pumps raise water 40 ft from a lake

FIG 6.14: *The Crofton pump house south of Marlborough which houses two massive working beam engines, one being the oldest in the world that is still in steam. These pumps draw water up from the nearby spring-fed lake known as Wilton Water. It is then discharged into an open channel which carries it just over a mile to the summit level.*

FIG 6.15: *A popular and busy canalside pub on the Caldon canal near Leek.*

up to the summit pound. At Lea Wood on the Cromford canal a steam pump lifts water from the river Derwent, and at Smethwick on the Birmingham system a restored engine lifts water from Telford's new main line, up to the old, higher, line. This engine is the last of 17 that once served the Birmingham canal network.

Canalside Pubs

A feature of virtually every canalside town or village, the pubs would provide stables to rest the towing horses and a meeting place for the boatmen. In addition, medical care would be available at some and many stocked provisions. You will often come across obvious waterway names like the Navigation, the Barge and Barrel, the Quays or the Tiller Pin. Today many make a virtue of their waterside location and offer a pleasant resting place on a towpath walk.

CHAPTER 7

The Boats

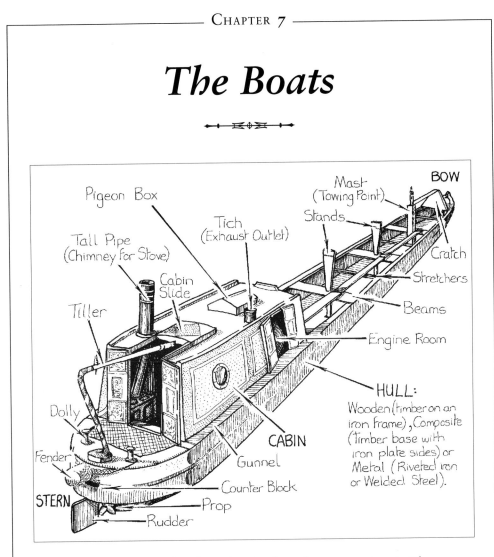

Pigeon Box

Tich
(Exhaust Outlet)

Tall Pipe
(Chimney for Stove)

Cabin
Slide

Tiller

Dolly

Fender

STERN

Rudder

Prop

Counter Block

Gunnel

CABIN

Mast
(Towing Point)

Stands

BOW

Cratch

Stretchers

Beams

Engine Room

HULL:
Wooden (timber on an
iron frame), Composite
(timber base with
iron plate sides) or
Metal (Riveted iron
or Welded Steel).

FIG 7.1: *Diagram of a working boat showing the main component parts. There were minor variations depending on the type of cargo or the area where the boat was built.*

Working Boats

For all but the last 50 or so years virtually the only boats on the canals were working boats. On the narrow canals these followed the 70 ft x 7 ft size with a cabin at the back. Up to the 1840s this cabin was purely a place for the boatmen to rest and

sleep whilst on long trips. It was probably fairly crude and largely undecorated. All these craft were pulled by a horse or sometimes mules or donkeys. On the wider canals and rivers the same principle applied but the cabins on these craft could sometimes be built under the decking

FIG 7.2: *A typical Fellows, Morton & Clayton working pair, returning unloaded. Note the forward cabin on the towed boat – used for the children, but not liked.*

rather than as a raised structure.

The decoration of the boats, which became a virtual art form, developed slowly. The original canal regulations required boats to display basic identification (see chapter 1) but early company craft would have had some decoration including the now familiar diamonds. These schemes were primarily to identify the company and proclaim their presence, and were used on both river and canal craft. It wasn't long before the carrying companies took the need to identify their craft to its logical end and

made the name and town occupy the entire cabin side as a form of advertising.

It is generally agreed that as the wives moved onto the boats from the mid 19th century, they improved on the internal decoration but we must remember that the boats were generally painted when in a boatyard for repairs or alterations, so the paint schemes were developed by the boatyard painter not the individual boater and his family.

The boats themselves changed little, the sizes had been set by the dimensions of the canal structures and apart from minor

FIG 7.3: *The beautifully restored horse drawn boat 'Ilkeston'. It is one of only a few horse drawn boats that have survived to be restored.*

changes to the underwater shape to get the best passage through the water, and the arrival of engines from the 1860s on, little altered over 250 years.

On the broad canals boats of up to 14 ft wide were built and though heavy work they could still be pulled by a single horse. They were of course limited to the wide canal network and rivers. Thus they became standard on canals like the Leeds & Liverpool, the Rochdale and the Kennet & Avon. Like most of the broad canals, these all connected with navigable rivers where the size of the craft was not a problem.

Construction

Originally the boats were built of timber planks on iron framing. Despite some experimental, all iron boats, tried out in 1787 and again in 1803, wood remained predominant until the arrival of steam power in the late 19th century. The curves at the bows and stern were created by putting the planks in steam chests where they would become pliable and then applying much brute force! By the time steam power had arrived the sides were often being made of iron plate, but still with a timber bottom, usually elm, known as composite construction. By the early 1900s boats were being made entirely of riveted iron and after around 1920 usually had diesel engines. Welded steel boats appeared after the Second World War and the very last working boats were built this way.

The living cabins had been added to

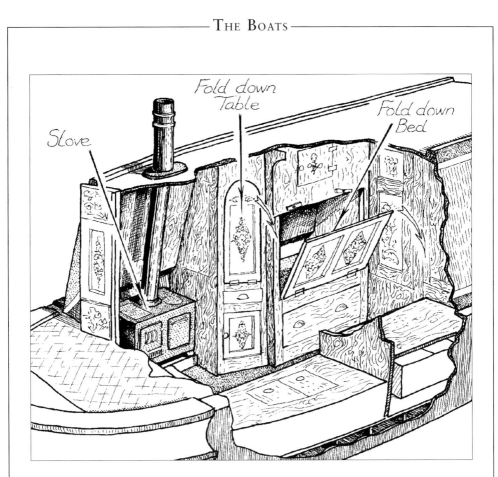

FIG 7.4: *Standard narrowboat living cabin. Built from fairly indifferent woods the interior would be scumbled to imitate wood grain. The interior would also be highly decorated with lace plates and ribbon work.*

existing boat designs and later (following the 1877 and 1884 Canal Acts) a small cabin was added to the front of the boat to make a bedroom for the children. All such cabin space reduced the cargo carrying space and was provided very begrudgingly by the owners.

Though the external paint schemes varied from company to company the cabin layout was remarkably standard. On narrowboats this layout had to be remarkable, for the family lived in an area of just 8 ft 6 inches long by 6 ft wide. Many functions like washing were performed outside, and due to the long working hours very little time was actually spent in the cabin apart from sleeping. Replicas of these cabins can be seen at the main boat museums. These only add to one's amazement that such a small space could house a family.

Engines

Experiments had been made to replace the

FIG 7.5: *A fully restored and decorated diesel engined working boat. These are referred to as the motor whilst the unpowered boat they tow is the butty.*

horse by mechanical engines of various types from as early as the 1790s. None proved acceptable and not until well into the 1800s did steam engine tugs appear which could tow boats along the rivers and more rarely the canals. On canals steam tugs found use in the longer tunnels where they replaced the onerous task of legging.

By the 1870s steam engines were being fitted into both broad and narrow canal boats and the towing of a second boat, or butty, started to become the norm. Both boats would have cabins but the butty was regarded as the home. These boats, however, didn't displace the majority of horse drawn craft. Their effect was interesting, though; on the Leeds & Liverpool canal a fleet of 30 steam engine boats displaced some 300 horses and were reckoned to save money, albeit only just. Inevitably diesel engines were introduced to replace steam early in the 20th century and this type of craft signalled the end of the horse drawn boat.

FIG 7.6: 'Modern' working boats delivering diesel fuel and coal. The motor is a restored Admiral class boat, an example of the last, all welded steel, working boats built.

Flyboats and Packet Boats

These were special types of boat developed to carry lighter loads at increased speed. The flyboats would run to timetables and carry up to 15 tons of goods. They travelled night and day to achieve short journey times. Packet boats, sometimes called swift or gig boats, carried passengers. By using a very fine shape and lightweight construction these craft could move faster through the water than normal craft and provided regular passenger services between many larger towns. Both had priority over all other craft at locks and bridges. Usually pulled by two horses, which were regularly changed, these services provided a safe and smooth passage at remarkable speed.

At first there was no highway code for the canals and rules were soon needed to control the boats, especially on the busy industrial sections. When one horse drawn boat passed another, someone had to give way and allow their towing rope to fall to

FIG 7.7: *Typical modern hire boat. These robust boats usually have all the normal modern comforts of home – provided you can cope with the 7 ft wide space.*

the bottom of the canal to enable the other boat to pass over it. Rules were drawn up as to which type of boat or cargo had precedence but often it came down to who shouted the loudest. Boats nearing locks would race to reach the lock and it was not unknown for fights to ensue to settle who was going through first. Marker posts were sometimes used on the approaches to locks – but who got to theirs first was still a source of controversy!

Restored working boats can still be seen at most of the canal museums and many proudly parade at the major national boat shows.

Pleasure Boats

Today the canals are used almost exclusively by modern pleasure narrowboats. At the start of leisure boating the most readily available boats were wooden or fibreglass river craft and indeed many still survive. The problem with such craft is that they are not too

FIG 7.8: *A typical modern day luxury pleasure boat.*

good at taking the inevitable knocks from locks and concrete canal edges. Keeping them warm and dry in our unreliable weather also tends to count against them. Taking a leaf from the last of the working boats built in the 1960s the leisure industry started using welded steel to produce tough little boats which were still affordable. Inevitably the market for longer and stronger boats grew and by the 1980s a mature industry had developed, building everything from small and cheap to strong and stylish boats with many working boat features. The hire boat industry too needed tough, reliable boats. Like so many pastimes the pleasure boat business has moved steadily upmarket and today's craft are generally in the 40 to 60 ft long range with all the normal facilities of home built in.

With one or two exceptions the hull is flat bottomed – usually 8 or 10 mm thick mild steel with sides in 6mm steel and the cabin constructed in 3 or 4 mm steel. The

FIG 7.9: *Bradford on Avon on the Kennet & Avon canal. The local trip boat has just ascended the lock and is getting ready to tie up at the wharf.*

shape of the bows is a point of pride with the best hulls making a very good copy of the graceful curves of the working boats. The rear underwater swim has a great effect on how smoothly the craft passes through the water with, again, the best hulls having the more complex and better shape.

Boats come with three types of stern; the cruiser style has a large open back and is popular with hire fleets, the traditional style attempts to mimic the working boats with only a small semi circle area behind the cabin, while the very popular 'semitrads' combine the external appearance of the 'trad' but with increased comfort for the crew, who can keep the

steerer company. It is worth noting that it is polite to refer to modern steel pleasure craft as narrowboats and not barges, which is rather like calling a BMW a lorry!

The engine – invariably diesel – normally resides close to the rear and drives a single propeller behind which is mounted the rudder. This is connected above the rear deck to the tiller which has an 'S' shape and often ends with much polished brass and decoration. These rudders and tillers are used on powered craft as the water is being driven into the rudder by the propeller, giving relatively good steering for a small rudder area. The horse drawn boats and the buttys,

FIG 7.10: *Market Drayton on the Shropshire Union canal. Once the site of an early boat sales company (Ladyline) it's now modern housing and moorings.*

however, had no such driven water and had to use a much larger area rudder (called an elum) in order to get a purchase against the slow moving water.

Very occasionally the engine is mounted away from the rear and drives the propeller by means of a hydraulic motor. Smaller craft often use an outboard engine which doesn't need a rudder since the entire engine and propeller is turned to steer the boat.

Most modern boats carry liquid petroleum gas (LPG) to fuel cooking, water heating and sometimes run the fridge. Strict regulations regarding its storage result in the cylinders being kept in compartments in the bows or at the rear where any leaked gas will flow overboard. LPG is heavier than air and will sink to the floor if it gets loose inside the boat. Unlike caravans you can't make a hole in the floor to clear it! The most striking aspect of these modern leisure boats is their paintwork, which along with the boat's name can be a source of endless joy.

The top of the range private boats often have a traditional living cabin at the rear, an engine room next and the rest of the boat's accommodation is built where once there would have been cargo. Old style, slow running diesel engines are prized amongst these seriously expensive craft.

The Trent & Mersey canal in Stone. This is Lime Kiln lock, reflecting one of the earliest cargoes carried by the canals.

Section III

What To See

CHAPTER 8

Visiting Canals

Walking the Canals

Generally the canal towpaths are in good order, though normal countryside walking footwear is wise away from the popular spots. If you would like to see general canal activity then head for one of the points where there is a group of locks or a junction between canals. At these spots towpaths are usually very good and pubs are never far away. Remember that boat movements are fairly thin on the ground during the maintenance season – November to March.

For longer distance walks remember that deep cuttings are often very wet and muddy – the Shropshire Union suffers this problem in both the Grub Street and Woodseaves cuttings south of Market Drayton, though the rest of the route is very rewarding. The Grand Union also suffers from wet paths at Shrewley tunnel. There are still one or two points where the towpath is either non existent or very difficult, though such sections are usually easy to bypass using local roads. Incidentally, most tunnels have well defined paths over them, originally intended for the horses but still in use for walkers.

Though legally most towpaths are not public rights of ways, virtually all are open to the public and their use is encouraged.

Museums and Boat Shows

For those who would like to sample more canal history I must mention the three main canalside museums. These are run by the recently created Waterways Trust.

The Boat Museum at Ellesmere Port, north of Chester, boasts a large collection of working boats and is a rich source of historical knowledge. The Manchester Ship canal passes the site though boat movements are not too common now that the commercial docks in Manchester have closed leaving mainly chemical cargos to Ellesmere Port and Runcorn.

The Canal Museum at Stoke Bruerne, near Daventry, has a smaller museum, a superb bookshop and is one of the most popular spots on the canal system for just watching the boats go by. There are also trip boats and just a gentle stroll north is the entrance to the Blisworth tunnel.

The National Waterways Museum at Gloucester Docks, set out in a beautifully restored warehouse, also houses many of the archive records of our canal heritage. Again the whole area is well worth a visit.

Boats of all types can be seen at one of the boat shows that are held each year on the canal system. By their very nature they move both in time and place, so if you fancy going to one, check the waterways magazines first.

The following are regular events but do check the dates:

Ellesmere Port, nr Chester: Easter
Little Venice, nr Paddington, London:
    May Day
Crick, between Rugby and
Northampton: Spring Bank Holiday
Braunston, nr Daventry: Spring Bank
    Holiday

National Indoor Arena, Birmingham: In July
Braunston, nr Daventry: August Bank
  Holiday
Inland Waterways Association National
  Festival (moves each year): August
  Bank Holiday

All these national shows are very popular,
often crowded and most make an entry
charge. Many feature restored working
boats as well as canal related stalls and
shows. There are also dozens of smaller
local events, many run by the IWA,
around the country. Again details can be
found in the magazines, in particular the
March or April issues.

In addition to the Waterways Trust sites
there is another important canalside
museum. The Black Country Museum
near Dudley, in Birmingham, is one of
several active museums that endeavour to
create the ambience of an earlier age. In
particular it features much canal related
activity including the restoration of old
working boats, and boat trips are also run
through the Dudley tunnel. This bore,
like Brindley's first Harecastle tunnel, is
small and without a towpath. One of the
trips includes the chance to try legging a
boat yourself plus passing through the
vast limestone caverns that were once
served by the canal.

Places to Visit

The following list gives the location of some of the features mentioned in the book.
Many have car parking, interpretation boards, visitor centres or shops.

Feature	Canal	Name	Location
Aqueduct	Kennet & Avon	Dundas	Nr Limpley Stoke, SE of Bath
Aqueduct	Kennet & Avon	Avoncliff	W of Bradford on Avon
Aqueduct	Peak Forest	Goyt or Marple	N of Marple
Aqueduct	Llangollen	Chirk	SW of Chirk
Aqueduct	Llangollen	Pontcysyllte	Trevor, twixt Chirk and Llangollen
Boat Lift	Trent & Mersey	Anderton	NW of Northwich
Boat Lift	Edinburgh & Glasgow	Falkirk Wheel	Falkirk
Inclined Plane	Grand Union	Foxton	NW of Market Harborough
Locks	Staffs & Worcs	Bratch	SW of Wolverhampton
Pumps	Kennet & Avon	Claverton	SE of Bath
Pumps	Kennet & Avon	Crofton	SE of Marlborough
Pumps	Cromford	Lea Wood	S of Matlock
Pumps	Birmingham Canal Network	Smethwick	N of Smethwick
Staircase Locks	Leeds & Liverpool	Bingley 5	Bingley
Staircase Locks	Shropshire Union	Northgate	Chester
Staircase Locks	Caledonian	Banavie	N of Fort William
Staircase Locks	Caledonian	Fort Augustus	Fort Augustus
Staircase Locks	Caledonian	Muirtown	Inverness

Places to see Boating Activity

Lock flights

Ashton	Ancoats to Openshaw, Manchester
Birmingham Canal Network	Farmers Bridge and Wolverhampton
Coventry	Atherstone
Grand Union	Marsworth, Buckby, Braunston, Stockton, Rothersthorpe
GU Leicester Branch	Watford and Foxton
Huddersfield	Most of the canal is heavily locked
Kennet & Avon	Crofton, Devizes and Bath
Leeds & Liverpool	Wigan, Wheelton, Blackburn, Barrowford and Bingley
Llangollen	Hurleston and Grindley Brook
Macclesfield	Bosley
Oxford	Napton and Hillmorton
Peak Forest	Marple
Rochdale	Todmordon, Summit
Shropshire Union	Adderley and Audlem
Staffs & Worcs	Bratch
Stratford upon Avon	Lapworth and Wilmcote
Trent & Mersey	Stone
Worcester Birmingham	Tardebigge

Junctions

Birmingham Canal Network	Broad Street, Birmingham
Coventry/Oxford	Hawkesbury
Coventry/Trent & Mersey	Fradley
Grand Union/Oxford	Braunston
Grand Union/Stratford	Lapworth
Leeds & Liverpool	Wigan
Macclesfield/Peak Forest	Marple
Shropshire Union/Llangollen	Hurleston
Staffs & Worcs/River Severn	Stourport
Staffs & Worcs/Shroppie	Autherley
Staffs & Worcs/Trent & Mersey	Great Haywood
Trent & Mersey/Macclesfield	Kidsgrove

GLOSSARY

'A' FRAME: Two frames, shaped like the letter A, the tops being joined by a strong bar from which block and tackle lifting gear can be used. Normally used to replace lock gate.

AQUEDUCT: A structure to carry a water channel over some other feature.

ARM: A short length of canal branching from a main route.

ASHES: Waste product from fires, used to seal leaking stop planks.

BEAM: The width of a boat or a straight structure designed to support weight.

BLACKSMITH: One who manufactures artefacts from iron.

BLOW LAMP: A device for burning paraffin or LPG to produce a controlled jet of flame.

BOATYARD: An area where boats can be built or repaired.

BOATMEN: The men who worked the boats.

BOLLARD: A stout circular post, usually no more than 2 ft high, used to secure ropes.

BOW: The front of a boat, specifically the way the hull narrows to a point.

BRITISH WATERWAYS: Government controlled organisation which runs most of the British canal system.

BROAD CANAL: Any canal with a structure width of over 7 ft 6 inches.

BUTTY: An unpowered boat towed by a powered boat.

BUTYL LINER: A sheet of modern synthetic rubber used to waterproof anything holding water.

CABIN: That part of a boat designed to house people.

CAISSON: A rectangular iron or steel box which can hold water and one or more boats.

CHAMBER: The part of a lock contained within the gates.

CHUTE: A sloping channel or pipe down which materials can be slid or dropped.

CONTOUR CANAL: A canal which follows a contour line in order to avoid cuttings or embankments.

CRATCH: A triangular board, usually decorated, mounted at the front of the boat and used to support the top planks and covers.

CRUISER: A pleasure boat. On canals the term is often reserved for wooden or fibreglass boats.

CULVERT: Tunnel or pipe used to carry water.

CUTTING: An open passageway dug through a hill to allow the canal to stay level.

DAM: A raised bank, usually of earth, to hold back water.

DEPOT: A building or area used to distribute goods.

DIESEL: A type of fuel, less volatile than petrol. Often loosely used to describe a boat which has a diesel engine.

DOCK: An enclosed area of water where boats can load or unload cargoes.

DOLLY: Term used to describe a short post or collar on the end of a lock gate around which a rope can be placed to open or close the gate.

DOUBLE LOCK: Two locks joined as a staircase, without a pound in between them.

DREDGING: Removing the accumulated silt and earth from a canal.

ELUM: The large wooden rudder on horse drawn boats or a butty. Sometimes spelt 'hellum'.

EMBANKMENT: A raised structure of earth and stone used to carry a canal above the ground level. The opposite of a cutting.

FIBREGLASS: A general term for glass reinforced plastic.

FLASH LOCK OR STAUNCH: An early method of permitting boats to pass through a weir or dam.

FLIGHT: A term used to describe a series of locks that are physically close together.

FLYBOATS: Lightweight boats which could travel faster than normal cargo boats. They could also travel at night.

FORD: A shallow crossing of a river where horses and carts could cross without damage to the goods they were carrying.

GATE: A structure to block access. Usually swung out of the way on hinges or pivots.

GIG: A type of rowing boat with a hull shape that was copied for canal passenger boats.

GRIST: The ground bones of animals.

GUILLOTINE: A vertically raised gate still common on the rivers of East Anglia.

HATCH: A rectangular lid which could slide or lift to gain access to a cabin.

HORSE DRAWN: A boat which was pulled along by a horse using a long towing rope.

HUNDREDWEIGHT: A twentieth part of a ton. Abbreviated to 'cwt'.

HYDRAULIC: Operated by fluid under pressure and carried in pipes.

INCLINED PLANE: A flat slope up which boats could be carried.

INDUSTRIAL REVOLUTION: General term referring to the period roughly between 1750 and 1820 when the mass production of goods in factories evolved.

INLAND WATERWAYS ASSOCIATION: A charitable organisation formed in 1948 to campaign for the restoration and well being of our canals and rivers.

INTERCHANGE BASINS: Canal basins interleaved with railway tracks where goods could be easily transferred between the two transport systems.

JUNCTION: The point where two or more canals joined.

KEY: Another term for the windlass used to operate lock paddle gear.

LEET: An artificial channel dug to direct river water to a water wheel.

LEGGING: The process of moving a boat through a tunnel by lying down on the boat and 'walking' along the walls.

LIFT: A device for lifting a boat from one level to another.

LIFT BRIDGE: Simple form of canal bridge which can be lifted up to allow boats to pass.

LINESMAN: Canal employee responsible for a stretch of canal.

LINING: Any waterproof layer applied to the canal channel to prevent water leakage.

LIQUID PETROLEUM GAS (LPG): An inflammable gas held in containers under pressure such that it turns to liquid. On release of the pressure it returns to a gaseous form.

LOCK: A structure which enables a boat to change level.

MARINA: General term for an area of water used to store boats; the site usually has commercial activities as well.

MAST: A vertical post to which the towing rope would be attached.

MASTER: The person in charge of a boat.

MILEPOST: Posts, often in cast iron, which give the distance to junctions or other significant places along the canal route.

MILL PONDS: The area of river water that would be created by a dam or weir placed across a river. Used to feed water wheels.

MOORINGS: A place where boats may be secured.

MOTOR: Name given to a canal narrowboat which has an engine and tows another unpowered boat.

NARROWBOAT: Canal boat with a width of 7 ft and a maximum length of 70 ft. Most modern narrowboats are built to a 6 ft 10 inches width to cope with some structures and locks that have narrowed over the years.

NARROW CANAL: Canal built to take boats 70 ft long by 7 ft wide.

NATIONALISATION: The process by which the government took ownership of the canals.

NAVVIES: Abbreviation of navigators, the term used for the men who dug and built the canals. The same men later moved to building the railways and it was then that the term was shortened to navvy.

NUMBER 1: A boatmen who owned his boat rather than working for a carrying company.

OUTBOARD: Term for a removable boat engine that is fitted outside the boat structure.

PACKET: Passenger carrying boat.

PACKHORSES: Horses used to carry goods along roads.

PADDLE: Square plate which covers an underwater opening. The paddle sits in guides and can be raised to allow the water to pass.

PADDLE AND RIMER: Parts of a flash lock or staunch. The paddles hold back the water and the rimers hold the paddles in place.

PAWL: Mechanical device that allows a gear or ratchet to rotate in one direction but not the other.

PILES: Planks of wood, concrete or steel which are driven into the banks of canals or rivers to form a stable edging.

PLANES: Inclined planes.

POLE: Sometimes called a shaft, this is the stout length of wood up to 12 ft long used to push boats.

POUND: The stretch of water between locks.

POUND LOCKS: The normal modern lock which contains the boat within a chamber.

PUDDLE: Clay or loam mixture which can be worked to produce a waterproof lining for the canal channel.

PUMP HOUSE: A building which houses water pumps.

RATCHET: A toothed wheel or rack which in conjunction with a pawl will permit movement in one direction only.

RESERVOIR: A lake, usually man made, which holds water used to feed canals.

RIMER: Guide frame used to hold paddles in old style weirs and flash locks.

ROLLER: A round length of wood mounted vertically which is able to turn.

ROSES AND CASTLES: Traditional early 19th century decoration.

RUDDER: Flat underwater structure at the rear of a boat which enables it to be steered.

SCUMBLE: A painting technique used to create an apparent even colour and grain in an otherwise poor quality piece of wood.

SHAFT: See pole.

SHUTTERING: Planks or sheets used to form the shape of a structure into which brickwork or concrete is laid, the shuttering being removed once the structure is complete.

SIDE PONDS: Brick or stone built ponds at the side of a lock, used to hold water.

SIDE POUNDS: Sections of canal used to increase the water area between locks in a flight.

SILT: Soft mud and soil which has washed into a water channel over several years and which restricts the passage of boats.

SLIPPAGE: Problem of canals built on a slope where the underlying soil starts to move down the slope, taking part of the canal with it.

SLUICE: A gate controlling a water channel, usually associated with handling excess or flood water.

STAIRCASE LOCKS: Locks built with no pound between them. The top gate of one lock becomes the bottom gate of the next lock.

STAUNCH: See flash lock.

STEAM CHESTS: A closed box filled by steam from a boiler used to soften wood prior to bending it to form the bows of a boat.

STOP PLANKS: Planks of wood which can be dropped into slots to build up a barrier across a canal. Used to allow sections of canal to be drained for repair work.

SUMMIT: A high point of a canal's route.

SWIM: The underwater shape of a boat, particularly the area leading to the propeller on engine driven craft.

SWING BRIDGE: A simple bridge structure which can be swung out of the way to allow boats to pass.

TAN PIN: The iron pin on the bottom of lock gates which forms the turning point for the gate.

THEODOLITE: Surveying instrument for measuring levels and angles.

TIE BARS: Iron or steel rods used to hold two masonry walls together.

TILLER: The pole by which the rudder is turned.

TOGGLE: A short piece of wood passed through a rope as a fastening device.

TOWING: The process of pulling a boat along using a rope attached to a horse or mule which walks along the towpath.

TOWPATH: The pathway alongside the canal originally used by the horses towing the boats.

TROLLEY: Misused word referring to the collection of electricity from wires in the roof of tunnels (similar to trams or trolley buses).

TUGS: Boats designed solely to pull or manoeuvre other boats.

TURNOVER BRIDGE: Bridge constructed to allow the towing horse to change from one side of a canal to the other without having to disconnect the towing rope.

TURNPIKE TRUSTS: Groups of people who were authorised to collect tolls from road users in return for using the money for the upkeep of the road.

TURN WHEEL: A hand wheel which is turned to control the speed of an engine.

UNDERSHOT: Type of water wheel where the wheel sits in the flow of a river rather than having the water poured over it.

WATERWAYS TRUST: The charitable body formed to run the canal museums and aid the restoration of derelict canals.

WATER WHEEL: Wheel turned by water, usually from a river, which in turn drives machinery.

WEIR: A controllable opening in a dam which permits control over the amount of water passing through the dam.

WHARF: Canal or riverside space where boats can load and unload. Often includes buildings associated with the boat goods.

WINCH: Mechanical device to wind a rope or cable.

WINDING: The process of turning a canal boat around to face the direction from which it has come.

WINDLASS: A cranked handle which is used to wind paddle gear up and down at locks. Sometimes called a key.

WORKSHOP: Group of buildings involved in the maintenance of the canal.

BIBLIOGRAPHY

Anthony Burton: *The Great Days of the Canals*
Neil Cossons: *BP Book of Industrial Archaeology*
Coventry Canal Society: *Coventry's Waterways*
Charles Hadfield: *British Canals*
Charles Hadfield: *The Canal Age*
Charles Hadfield: *World Canals*
Charles Hadfield: *Canals of the East Midlands*
Charles Hadfield: *Canals of the West Midlands*
John A. Hill: *From Stem to Stern*
A.J. Lewery: *Narrow Boat Painting*
Hugh McKnight: *The Shell Book of Inland Waterways*
Edward Paget-Tomlinson: *The Illustrated History of Canal & River Navigations*
L.T.C. Rolt: *Navigable Waterways*
Ronald Russell: *Lost Canals of England and Wales*
Ray Shrill: *Birmingham's Canals*

Current waterways magazines
Waterways World: 01283 742970
Canal Boat and Inland Waterways: 01189 771677
Canal and Riverboats: 01372 741411

WATERWAY ORGANISATIONS

British Waterways:
Web site: www.britishwaterways.co.uk
Customer Service Centre: 01923 201120

The Inland Waterways Association
Web site: www.waterways.org.uk
01923 711114

The Waterways Trust
Web site: www.thewaterwaystrust.co.uk

The Boat Museum, Ellesmere Port: 01513 555017

The Canal Museum, Stoke Bruerne: 01604 862229

The National Waterways Museum, Gloucester: 01452 318054

L

Leeds and Liverpool canal 18, 24, 60, 108, 110
legger, legging 92, 119
lifts 30, 69–70
lining 40–41
Liverpool 16, 24
lock gates 35, 53, 57
locks 16, 50–64
  double 64
  flash or staunch 13–14, 26
  pound 14–15, 55
  staircase 60, 61, 64
Llangollen canal 40, 58, 61, 76, 78, 86–87
London North Western railway 28
Loughborough navigation 22

M

Macclesfield canal 20, 76
maintenance 48
Manchester Ship canal 30, 118
motorised boats 30, 109–110, 114–115

N

narrowboat 19, 24, 106, 114
narrow canal 16
nationalisation 30

National Waterways Museum 118
navigation rules 111–112
Neptune's Staircase 64
New Junction canal 30
Number 1s 29

O

Oxford canal 30, 37, 41, 60, 74, 76, 77, 95, 96, 100

P

packet boat 111
paddle 51–56
Peak Forest Canal 72, 84, 85
Pickford of Manchester 22, 24
piling 42, 43–44
pound lock. See locks
pump houses 100–105
  Claverton 100, 103
  Crofton 103, 104, 105
  Lea Wood 105
  Smethwick 105

R

railway interchange basin 27
railways 20, 24
  impact of, 28, 34
repair techniques 41, 42, 43–44, 49
river navigation 13–15
road transport, impact of, 30

Rochdale canal 108
Rushall canal 20

S

Severn canal 18
Severn river 19
Shropshire Union 20, 115, 118
side ponds 58–60
signs 97–100
Stoke Bruerne Canal Museum 118
Staffs & Worcs canal 58, 63
stop gate, 45, 47
stop plank 45–47
staircase lock. See locks
staunch lock. See locks
Stratford upon Avon canal 76, 77, 79
swift boat 111

T

Tame Valley canal 20
Telford, Thomas 20, 21, 24, 86
Thames canal 18
Thames river 13, 14, 26
towpaths 41, 43–44, 48, 87–88, 118
Trent and Mersey canal 10, 20, 41, 70, 73, 80, 92, 96, 97, 99, 116
tunnels 16–17, 20, 21, 87–92, 118
  construction 88–89, 92